THE
REDISCOVERY
OF THE
FRONTIER

✦

THE UNIVERSITY OF CHICAGO PRESS
CHICAGO, ILLINOIS

———

THE BAKER & TAYLOR COMPANY
NEW YORK

THE CAMBRIDGE UNIVERSITY PRESS
LONDON

THE MARUZEN-KABUSHIKI-KAISHA
TOKYO, OSAKA, KYOTO, FUKUOKA, SENDAI

THE COMMERCIAL PRESS, LIMITED
SHANGHAI

THE REDISCOVERY OF THE FRONTIER

By

PERCY H. BOYNTON

THE UNIVERSITY OF CHICAGO PRESS
CHICAGO · ILLINOIS

FOREWORD

✦

Early census returns in the spring of 1930 announced that Oklahoma City had a population of over 184,000. Edna Ferber's *Cimarron*, a best-seller of this same spring, looked back only forty years to the spectacular transformation of Indian Territory into Oklahoma. Both the census returns and the popular novel served as reminders that the opening of this district marked the closing of the frontier. Yet this reminder could be given only to the historians and other students who already knew that the frontier had always been significant in American life, and never more so than in its disappearance. Most of the country is still indifferent to the fact. Millions of ostensibly educated easterners lump everything beyond Pittsburgh and Buffalo into an indeterminate West. In 1928 they found that they had nothing to fear from it politically; a potential reason for understanding it was withdrawn; on that score the East did not need to puzzle over it any longer.

But, there is another something about the West that is more popularly intriguing than its politics. It is immensely, romantically picturesque; its human picturesqueness has been very real and very American and is still very recent. Since the close of the World War and the general revival of American self-consciousness and self-examination, a wave of interest in the postfrontier has been registered in the publication of an extraordinary lot of books. America, in the mood of John Milton on having arrived at the age of twenty-three, is startled by the fact of suddenly achieved maturity. Perhaps the semblance may deceive the truth; but time, the subtle thief, has stolen on the country, and the discovery that its youth is gone has turned it to retrospection as well as to introspection and circumspection.

In a time so filled with inquiry as to what America is and with speculation as to what the United States may become, such a turn of public attention is interesting. It may be negligible and it may be significant, but it raises various kinds of questions that call for answers. One would like to know, for instance, when and how the resurgence of attention to the frontier took shape and—far more difficult—why it occurred. One would like to know whether the treatment of the critics and biographers and novelists accords with the newer interpretations of the historians. And one cannot resist a temptation —which has been too strong for the historians themselves—to ask whether the passing of the frontier will result in a total decline of its influence, or whether the heritage from the frontier will be a rich and permanent bequest to the America of the future.

CONTENTS

✢

CHAPTER I

THE FRONTIER COMES OF AGE

❧

No DISCUSSION of the frontier can go far today without acknowledging that Frederick J. Turner gave the impulse for its general contemporary study. The inquisitive can easily find plenty of vague predecessors. But he must search far to find one better than the Nathaniel Ames, almanac-maker, who included in his issue for 1758, "A THOUGHT *upon the* past, present, *and* future State *of* North America." He concludes his first section, of less than two hundred words upon the past, with, "We know how the *French* have erected a Line of Forts from the *Ohio* to *Nova Scotia*, including all the inestimable Country to the West of us, into their exorbitant Claim.—This, with infinite Justice, the *English* resented, & in this Cause our

9308

Blood has been spill'd: Which brings to our Consideration,

"II. Secondly, The Present State of NORTH AMERICA.—A Writer upon this present Time says, 'The Parts of *North America* which may be claimed by *Great Britain* or *France* are of as much Worth as either Kingdom.—That fertile Country to the West of the Appalachian Mountains (a String of 8 or 900 Miles in Length,) between *Canada* and the *Mississippi*, is of larger Extent than all *France*, *Germany* and *Poland;* and all well provided with Rivers, a very fine wholesome Air, a rich Soil, capable of producing Food and Physick, and all Things necessary for the Conveniency and Delight in Life: in fine, 'the Garden of the World!' Time was when we might have been possess'd of it: At this Time two mighty Kings contend for this inestimable Prize . . . . —If we do not join Heart and Hand in the common Cause against our exulting Foes, but fall to disputing among ourselves, 'We shall have no Priviledge to dispute about, nor country to dispute in.'

"III. Thirdly, of the Future State of

NORTH AMERICA— .... The Curious have observ'd, that the Progress of Humane Literature (like the Sun) is from the East to the West; thus it has travelled thro' *Asia* and *Europe*, and now is arrived at the Eastern Shore of *America*. As the Coelestial Light of the Gospel was directed here by the Finger of G O D, it will, doubtless, finally drive the long! long! Night of Heathenish Darkness from *America:*—So Arts and Sciences will change the Face of Nature in their Tour from Hence over the Appalachian Mountains to the Western Ocean. O! Ye unborn Inhabitants of America! Should this Page escape its destined Conflagration at the Year's End, and these Alphabetical Letters remain legible,—when your Eyes behold the Sun after he has rolled the Seasons round for two or three Centuries more, you will know that in Anno Domini 1758, we dream'd of your Times."

Events moved farther and faster than the almanac-maker dreamed. Four generations later an American historian was citing an American census report which celebrated the passing of the frontier line and the closing of a great historic movement. It was because the chapter was closed but the pages were still legible as those of Nathaniel Ames that Turner urged the study of the western advance, the men who grew up under it, and the varied results in the community. For a quarter of a century he followed his own behest. Many others fell into line. The *Mississippi Valley Historical Review* became the organ for frontier historians; and by 1924, in the natural course, a successor of Turner's, Frederic Paxson, was ready with his *History of the American Frontier*. This is an exhaustive, circumstantial summary of events, a historian's effort to relate happenings rather than to interpret them, certainly rather than to force them into any formula. One more step remained. Turner had enunciated a theory in 1893. Paxson had synthesized the findings of a generation of scholars in 1924. In 1930 Paxson presented in a little volume, *When the West Is Gone*, his own thought on the past, present, and future of America in terms of the frontier.

Turner's original task was not simply to call attention to the western frontier: his undertaking was to define it and to interpret it. Two presumptions limit his discussions and those of all his disciples and probably save them from a complexity that would result in almost total confusion: First, that the frontier is conceived of from the English and Anglo-colonial point of view. The surviving nation is prevailingly English; its winning of the West was a conquest over primitive Americans no more than it was over French and Spanish colonizing forces; and it is always viewed through English eyes. Second, that of all types of pioneer, the farmer was so much the most constructive in his work and the most influential in his assertion of claims that the story of the frontier is chiefly the story of the frontier farmer. Yet even with these limitations the definition of the frontier developed a series of meanings like a series of interfitting Japanese boxes.

First and simplest is the use employed by the superintendent of the Census for 1890: the line, somewhere toward the west, of the territory owned by the United States on the sunset side of which the population was less than two to the square mile. From decade to decade this wavering line flowed across the continent until in 1890, though there were arid regions of underpopulation left, there was no line to be drawn short of the Pacific Coast. A second element in the definition, with deep implications, is that in its westering progress the frontier line always lay just eastward of the free lands; a third, that it was the boundary between savagery and civilization; and a fourth, that with variations determined by the nature of the regions, pioneering progressed in the regular order of explorer, then trapper and trader, then ranchman, farmer or miner, then of the full-fledged industrial community. All of which, taken in itself, is clear and not particularly thrilling.

But when Turner came to his interpretation of the frontier, thus defined, he set in motion probably the most exciting single idea that has ever been injected into the study of American history. This was that the experience of possessing and occupying and transforming a frontier was an enormously important determinant in American life. First of all, it transformed the pioneer himself; he became a new type of American while he was making a new America. Beyond this, moreover, the new country and the new occupant of it never quite lost the effect of the experience when the frontier moved westward. Then the West became an urgent claimant upon the eastern portions of the United States. It consolidated the whole country against Indians and foreign powers, determined economic legislation, promoted democracy in operation, and contributed to the national character the elements of energy, resourcefulness, and self-confidence that do most to differentiate the American from the European.

The use of this historical approach as a background for the current literary treatment of the frontier demands an acquaintance with certain obvious constants in the equation that are familiar to all students of history: what the American physical frontier has been; what the frontier processes have been; and what have been the social and political results of the frontier experience.

1. The physical frontier began, naturally, with the Atlantic Coast, when the first European settlers, prevalently English, tried to get a foothold there. At the end of a century and a half of effort there was a string of more or less isolated settlements from Massachusetts to Georgia, and between them and the mountains a new frontier, which served at once as a zone of escape for the poor and the discontented and as a buffer between the townsmen and the Indians. This was the first "West" as seen by colonists who had now established an East of their own.

The tide once started was not to stop as long as there was free land or cheap land to be occupied. The rivers flowing from the west furnished highways and disclosed the passes to the hinterland of the Appalachian valleys. Common hardships begot common interests among the pioneers, and these were deepened by a feeling of common resentment at the indifference of the older regions. By the end of the French and Indian War the vanguard were drifting down the westward slopes into the valleys of the Ohio, the Cumberland, and the Tennessee.

In 1763 an English proclamation forbade granting any further lands "west of the rivers flowing east," with no more deterrent effect on the migration than if it had prohibited the setting of the sun beyond a given longitude, and with the positive effect of stimulating the imaginations of frontiersmen and speculators alike. The wave of migration was spreading into the nearer reaches of the Mississippi Valley. The settlers came into a new kind of country. They were getting away from the thickly forested land, from fighting Indians behind trees to encountering them on horseback, away from the region of the log cabin to the region of the sod hut, and always farther from the East.

The impulse to push on westward was restimulated by the duresses of the embargo and the prolonged discomforts that accompanied the War of 1812. Kentucky, Tennessee, and Ohio were already admitted to the

Union. Between 1816 and 1821 five new states were enrolled: Indiana, Mississippi, Illinois, Alabama, and Missouri.

Mexico was now to south and west, and a wall of Indian reservations barred off all of the Louisiana Territory beyond Arkansas, as well as Missouri, Iowa, northern Illinois, and much of Wisconsin. But this was desirable farming and grazing land; the years from 1825 to the panic of 1837 saw the Indians thrust back, Wisconsin and Iowa opened up to occupation, and Arkansas admitted to statehood. The Mississippi Valley on both sides of the river was white man's country, and the frontier was creeping toward the Rockies.

Then came the discovery of gold, and the creep became a rush. The pot at the end of the rainbow was too alluring for the slow progression of former years. Overland and by water, the gold-seekers made their way, leaving the frontier line still far to the eastward, with a vast gap of unoccupied land and an ominous stretch of desert in the interval. Then in the late fifties prospectors working back from the coast found traces of gold in Colorado; and in the years of the Civil War the last stretch of prairie was overswept, the mineral resources were discovered in the high plains between the Rockies and Sierras, and settlement spread into the vast mountain states. In the meanwhile Texas had been annexed, and the territories of New Mexico and Arizona made the connecting link to California.

The outline sketch of the mere physical frontier epic contains only a few more major features. Between 1865 and 1890 the lands were thrown open to settlers and the free areas subject to government grant were all dispensed to schools and colleges, to railroads, and to individual homesteaders. Between 1865 and 1885 the grazing country was developed for open use and the cowboy ranger came into being, only to be largely superseded as barbed wire made inclosure possible and the extension of the railroads reduced the necessity of the long drives to the terminals. By 1890 the call of free land was over; the rush into Oklahoma was a memory;

the story of the frontier was awaiting its chroniclers, and the significance of the frontier its interpreters.

2. On this succession of frontiers there has been a regular procedure of social evolution. After the explorers and the trappers and traders, came the settlers with their first problems of clearing fields and building shelters and their next ones of establishing working relationships among themselves. They brought social traditions which they found either satisfactory or in need of modification or abandonment. And they brought also a technique of settlement which had to be adapted to the nature of the region they entered, shifting from forest to prairie and from prairie to high plain. When the farms were operable, when neighborhoods were established, and town organization was in force, roads, schools, churches and courts followed, and the district was no longer in the foremost zone. It was become a passageway to the extreme frontier and was supplying some of the youth and some of the incorrigibly restless elders who were impelled to follow the sun.

This secondary frontier was due for further transformation. For a while it was on the line of communication: it passed on supplies and it caught the returning news. It shared the temper of the zone beyond it, depending like the newest region on the country to the East for fresh recruits, for basic supplies, for financial support, and for the market at which to recoup its fortunes. But in time it was replaced by another secondary frontier. As it fell back to the third or fourth or fifth wave, a new tide began to overflow it—the tide of industrialism. It became the middle-man's region and, on the whole, a creditor's region. As its memories of the frontier receded, it looked back to a recent heritage; but it looked around itself to anything but frontier conditions. It might be located in an agricultural area, but it was become a city of banks and merchants and manufacturers. It read the crop reports, but it followed the stock exchange too. Today the channel of financial security must be followed between the Scylla of farm mortgages and the Charybdis of brokers' loans. The post-frontier cherishes a sentimental regard for the farmer and his wheat field, but it listens with respectful deference to the opinions of Wall Street.

3. From the frontier regions and the frontier processes the historians have led on to their main subject: the significance of the frontier in American history. They point out that from the beginning to the end of the pioneering days, the movement was impelled by poverty, manned by youth, buoyed by hope, and maintained by hard and unremitting labor. Assets of these kinds were not open to quantitative measurement. They were equalitarian in essence, for any pioneer could have as much of any of them as his own nature would allow. They did not depend on any theory of democracy, but they produced democracy in fact. This democracy in fact led to impatient resentment at any assumption of superiority whether on the frontier or in the older country. And whatever traits the selective process emphasized in the recruiting of the frontier army were reinforced by the actual frontier life. Those who lacked

courage and persistence stopped on the way or returned. Those who could not endure the hardships died. Primitive conditions subjected humankind to the brutal tests of survival of the fittest, through brute strength or through adaptation; and the survivors naturally retained in heightened degree the qualities that the frontier demanded and begot.

People of this stock naturally believed in social progress and in their own power to contribute to it by mastering the land and enriching themselves at the scene of their conquest. And people of this experience realized that life had taught them things about their own needs and rights that the older country must be convinced of. In this broadening empire they were being accepted not as colonials but as members in a federation with full prerogatives and well-developed vocal powers. An ignorant and complacent and provincial East was not to be left in its ignorance and complacency. The West was aware of clearly developed sectional differences; and the East, early conscious of dangers, spoke of the pioneers as "idle," "talkative," "passionate," "prodigal," "shiftless," "impatient of restraint," and feared their influence on national policies as their representation was increasing in Congress. Well it might, for the frontier had developed a new type of American with a new and aggressive approach to national life.

These people who had been unified by common experiences, problems, and needs were urgent and incessant in their demands for legislation that would assist in the development of the West, and relentless in their assumption that the government was under obligations to help them. According to the historians, the government policies with regard to land, tariff, and internal improvements all originated in frontier ideas and needs. So did our foreign policies during the period of territorial expansion. And so, too, did the actual promotion of democratic ideas and, whether for better or for worse, of democratic social experiments. This is the gospel according to Turner.

And according to Paxson, the effects of western aggression can be clearly traced in five revolts of pioneer liberalism. First was the uprising against the English Tories, headed by George Washington, rebel and patriot. The second was the revolt of Thomas Jefferson, who looked to the Appalachian frontier for support while he challenged as dangerous to the liberties of the people every measure that Hamilton proposed and Washington indorsed. The third revolt was based on the "American system" of economic control, western in inception, propounded by Henry Clay in behalf of the native producer and carried to victory under the leadership of Andrew Jackson of Tennessee. The fourth revolt came to its height under Abraham Lincoln, of Illinois. "In the generation that ends at Gettysburg and Vicksburg, the South ceased to be the West . . . . but the West stayed West. It was as West that it gave Clay his elements for constructive thought. It was equally as West that it produced that revival of Jeffersonian equalitarianism that we know as Jacksonian democracy. . . . .

And it was still as West that, when later Jacksonians made and solidified their political alliance with the South, the newer borders of the West produced another appeal to human rights . . . . gave birth to the Kansas-Nebraska schism, and brought into existence a new Republican Party."

Then came the fifth great revolt of the agrarian West and the first one to fail. It took shape in 1896, three years after Turner's first declaration as to the significance of the frontier in American history, and, far from discounting this significance, emphasized it. For with the exhaustion of free land the generative power of the frontier was depleted, and the rising power of industrialism was at hand to check its momentum. It was like the revolts that had preceded it in springing from the needs of the farm area and in assuming that these needs were national in character. The men who had broken the western sod and were feeding the nation with a surplus for the outer world were debtors to the East as theretofore; but they had a new grievance against their creditors, as well as urgent necessity for piling up new liabilities.

Their grievance was against the railroad. There had been no redress against the menace of the sky. Heat and cold, drought and flood, prairie fire and locust plague, were acts of God. There was no corrective legislation against the vicissitudes of nature. But the voter could reach the railroad and the corporation that owned it. Their carrying charges were felt by the farmer on everything he bought and sold. They had gained vast acreages in free grants along their rights of way; they had been greedy and rapacious in demands and tactics. And every one of their offenses had been magnified under the slow-growing resentments of the homesteaders.

In the meanwhile the farmers' added need for capital came with the invention of the farm machinery, by means of which addition of debt resulted in multiplication of output, but without certain multiplication of proceeds. The cards seemed to be stacked against the farmer; all the capital seemed to be in the East, and Clay's American system of protection seemed to help the man who owned the factory at the expense of the man who owned the soil. So the farmer tried to turn economist, founded the Populist movement, captured the Democratic party in 1896, chose William Jennings Bryan as leader, and went down to defeat with him. From the western point of view, "Nothing is abnormal about the Populist revolt except its end. It lost. It failed to repeat a process of success that had been so often repeated that it might almost be assumed."

East and West had long been clearly demarked, but never had the clash of conflicting interests been anything like so clear. The earlier revolts had been based largely on political and economic theory, and the theory had ostensibly included the whole country. Henry Clay had devised his American system as a modus of defying the outer world. The West had been embarrassed by the unsold surplus of the farmer; the East, by indebtedness to foreign capitalists and competition with foreign industry. A protection of infant industries had therefore been calculated to put the eastern manufacturer on his feet and so establish a market for western commodities. The result, however, in the long run, had been to make the East the creditor of the West and to make the West pay for the protected commodities of the East without any comparable protection for the increasing product of the prairies.

By the time, then, of the Populist revolt and the attempt to solve the farmer's problem by a modification of the currency, the farmer was certain of his ills but only vaguely certain as to the remedy proposed by the Democratic standard-bearers; but the manufacturer was certain of his prosperity and equally certain of disaster with the adoption of Free Silver. The manufacturer saw to it that the wage-earner was apprised of the danger; so that the industrial East, employer and employed, stood for the protection of the full dinner-pail. Fear was more of an incentive than hope: fear could express itself more definitely, and fear had an immensely longer purse to draw upon in the expensive procedure of political campaigning. The West not only lost the revolt but lost the last chance for carrying at one stroke a new policy into effect and a new party into power. With the frontier gone, the old possibility of differentiating East and West waned just when the issue between them was theoretically more clear cut than it ever had been before.

Here, one is tempted to say, the matter rests, which is of all things what it does not do. The life of the country still depends on sun, cloud, and soil and on the husbandman. If Paxson's bold title *When the West Is Gone* carries its fair implications, it implies only a change in the conflict, not an ending of it. It may no longer be West against East, but it is more than ever the rural against the urban. When in 1928 the farm states supported a party that had not supported them, they repudiated a champion from "the sidewalks of New York." Roads and radios, motor cars and movies, bring the farmer into closer touch with the town, only to stress his isolation by increasing his wants without filling his purse. Flood control may some day be more than a project and a promise, and drought less of a menace. Whether benevolent legislation will ever be beneficent in effect is not so clear.

In the semi-arid regions still being reclaimed for settlement, all the pioneering processes are being carried on in miniature: the breaking of land and building of homes; the accumulation of debt in the wait for first returns; the utter subjection of the women to the sometimes futile, sometimes practical, enterprise of the men; the failure of the many who fertilize the land in travail for their successors; the varying successes of the few. And in the Middle-North the immigrant farmer on top of all this suffers the further duress of adjusting himself to a new world in which he is never more than a semi-alien and in which the children become alienated from the parents as they are assimilated into the country of their parents' choice.

So, though the frontier may have ceased to be an active determinant in national life, the farmer still prolongs the life of the pioneer—heir to his hardships if not to his hopes. Yet in spite of all, and with a buoyant optimism inherent in the subject of their studies, both Turner and Paxson contend that out of the West are still to come the essentially American contributions to the life of the twentieth century. It is a comfortable thought even though, mothered by the history of the frontier, it seems so clearly fathered by a wish.

There is a great deal of printed material—not to call it all literature—about the frontier and the pioneer, and a very great deal that was printed before the present retrospective outburst. Of the matter that was contemporary with the event, some that was unconscious and genuinely self-revealing appeared in unliterary publications and has only recently come in for critical attention. In its day the polite ignored it or apologized for it. The conscious literature of frontier days was of two main kinds: what was written from frontier communities—almost invariably affected, unrevealing of anything except the desire of the writers to compose the kind of thing approved by tradition; and what was written about the frontier by more or less careless and more or less unscrupulous observers and sojourners who put in writing a sentimentalized and rapidly conventionalized account to be marketed in the older country.

All this output becomes the subject of one class of contemporary books—the books about the literature of the frontier, some of them richly informative, others inclining to such neat interpretations of the frontier in terms of literature that they become formulas imposed on the past rather than deductions drawn from it. Another group, and a very voluminous one, is composed of retrospective portraits and studies, usually interesting, usually misleading when written to prove something, and at their best when their authors are content to deal with facts and leave the derivable theories to the intelligent reader.

The best material—and the nearest, of course, to pure literature—is the recent narrative. The novels of the native pioneer, truly told; the novels of the immigrant pioneer; and the supplementary biographies which emphasize, as good biography always does, how little there is to choose between fact and fiction—these carry along an epic cycle which is concluded with the fact and fiction of the backtrailers who seek in the older country the contentment in life that their forebears had hoped for in the West. It is with these various kinds of books that the following chapters are concerned.

CHAPTER II

THE FRONTIER IN LITERARY CRITICISM

✧

THE American literary critics and historians of today are headed by men and women
who came into their own after 1900. While
they were maturing, they were finding that
the United States was a world-power without a clear personality. It had fallen into im-
perial ways, but the emperor was as acci-
dental and colorless as many a recent czar or
king or president. John Macy, looking at
American literature with his own eyes, ob-
served that it was an "American province of
the empire of British literature," and asked
whether its provincialism was definable and
whether it was a virtue or a vice. Van Wyck
Brooks, after surveying the same array of authors, gazed beyond the literature to the
country that generated it, and concluded that

· 27 ·

America was "a prodigious welter of unconscious life, swept by ground-swells of half-conscious emotion." Each took the literature that was traditionally accepted, attempted a rediagnosis, threw out a challenge. And in the less than two decades since then, more has been done in restudying the nature and history of the American mind than in the two centuries that preceded. A statement of mine in those same years on "the American neglect of American literature" is a quaint relic of the past. This is no longer among America's sins of omission.

There have appeared many-volumed series of histories in complete review—histories of the novel, of the stage, of the drama, of the poetry, of the criticism; there have been revivals of neglected authors accompanied with multiplying biographies and reprints; there have been local studies, type studies, period studies; there have been abridgments of voluminous works, "hearts" of journals, reprints of inaccessible classics in a series of competing series, and anthologies by the shelfful of poetry, short story, play, long and short, and essay, critical and miscellaneous.

In the re-inventorying of the past there have been as many kinds of reactions as there have been kinds of reagents. The situation has been engagingly humanized to the point at which a study of the predispositions of the critics becomes quite as important as a knowledge of the subjects on which they are writing. In fact, it is the predispositions rather than the subject matter that have provided the discussion. For the man with a bee in his bonnet the bee is the most urgent fact in his immediate life; he feels that it is pertinent to any subject; if it is not, he does not shrink from unpertinence or impertinence. So the Puritans and the Victorians have been studied, analyzed, assailed, defended, excommunicated, canonized, mocked, and eulogized. The New Englanders have suffered for the sins of their ancestors. Poe, Whitman, and Melville have been triumphantly held up to view at the cost of the generations which neglected them; Hearn, Bierce, Crane, and Norris are beginning to profit in like fashion. In the course of the argument the preconceptions of whole generations turn out to be the most important element of all. Compare what the 1890's assumed and what the 1930's have to say about such formulas as the nobility of womanhood, the authority and wisdom of the parent, the dignity of labor, the glory of war, freedom of speech, or such provocative terms as "liberty," "democracy," "patriotism," and you will see that Van Wyck Brooks's wish for the "necessary contraposition of forces" that will define issues and determine values is by way of being fulfilled.

This revaluation of the best that has been written in the United States is a natural culmination of a century and a half of national self-consciousness. Youngsters like Freneau and Brackenridge, graduating from Princeton in 1770, and John Trumbull, taking his Master of Arts degree from Yale in the same year, began to project a cultural independence while they were still political provincials. From then on, the refrain was continually recurrent. But in spite of the long succession of protests, little came in the way of performance; and the little that was genuinely and indubitably indigenous was the literature of the unliterary. Among the gentry the tradition of the gentle reader was undisturbed; the only literature for them was polite literature. The *North American* and the *Knickerbocker* and the *Southern Literary* and *Harper's* and the *Atlantic* and *Russell's* and the *Galaxy* all gave it the stamp of approval. Some of these and many other periodicals clipped and printed it without payment to English authors; but none of them printed Walt Whitman. Whitman, the native product whom nobody read, and Beadle's dime novels, the native product which all the nobodies read, had alike to wait for posthumous critical recognition. It was quite natural. It is the way of youth, national or individual, to talk big, smoke behind the barn, and follow the fashions in public.

When a man like Cooper took violent issue with the ways of the hour, he was vilified and contemned: for long years no respectable publisher would risk a Whittier volume; Emerson was on the Harvard black list for nearly thirty years; Thoreau's essay on *Civil Disobedience* was discreetly overlooked; Hawthorne's *Scarlet Letter* was almost completely ignored in contemporary criticism, and Melville's output, until seventy years later. The Civil War did not awaken America from the prolonging of a British tradition to the development of an American one, for in spite of the flurry with Great Britain it did not involve any international challenge. There was nothing stimulative in the deadening return to normalcy that ensued. But the Spanish War and the sense of strength that came with it started new impulses that the World War was to release.

So there has followed a time of national introspection due with America's coming of age. There has been a vogue for the historical novel, a boom market for immigrant autobiographies—Schurz, Riis, Carnegie, Mary Antin, Bok, McClure, Pupin, Lewisohn; another for lives of native sons and daughters—Barnum, Jim Fiske, Beecher, Susan Anthony; and with these have come the decade books, starting with *The Fabulous For-*

ties and ending with the "mauve" nineties. In the midst of this surging activity the literary folk from time to time have borrowed the more inviting formulas of the physician and the psychologist, the economist and the political scientist, pursuing some of them as faddishly as new slang in current speech. Psychoanalysis in biography has spread to epidemic proportions; the economic interpretation of history, likewise. And few ideas or catchwords have proved to be more alluring than "the frontier."

Whether it was a matter of mere unaccountable coincidence, the result of a single influence, or the spirit of the times vaguely at work, there was from 1925 to 1927 a sudden outpouring of various kinds of books on the frontier. Three of these were definite pieces of literary history: one on the Middle West to 1840, when it ceased to be a frontier; one on the prairie up to the present; and the third, written on the Pacific Coast, on the whole subject of the frontier in American letters.

Mr. Rusk's *Literature of the Middle Western Frontier* is in many respects a model piece of work. It is voluminous, circumstantial, accurate in fact, discriminating in judgment, and complete in its equipment of scholastic accessories. The reader who cares to pursue a suggestion or to challenge one is given all the clues, and is forthwith disarmed by them. In the assembling caravan of new literary pioneers, the author seems to have been an unconscious leader. Just before the literary frontier came into fashion he studied the district where he was living. The name of F. J. Turner appears only in footnotes which do not allude to the historian's famous frontier thesis. Yet the Rusk book is momentous in the literary revival of the subject.

The chief deduction to be drawn from its marshaling of facts is that, with the rarest of exceptions, literature about the frontier is likely to be more genuinely authentic than the formal literature of the frontier. And the reason—Mr. Rusk does not explicitly state either fact or reason—is perfectly obvious. When the frontier begins to put itself on paper, it has ceased to be the habitat of the pioneer. It is becoming back country. It is self-consciously taking its pen in hand to address the gentle reader. The district may be satisfied with being rough and ready, but the element in it that wants to read and write wants also to be polite and sophisticated. And so it was, except for stray bits of balladry, the tall story, and odd excursions into newspaper humor, a hundred years ago in the Middle West.

Mrs. Trollope was bearing testimony to this polite quality in the current journalism when she wrote, "Every American newspaper is more or less of a magazine, wherein the merchant may scan, while he holds out his hand for an invoice, 'Stanzas by Mrs. Hemans,' or a garbled extract from 'Moore's Life of Byron'; the lawyer may study his brief faithfully, and yet contrive to pick up the valuable dictum of some American critic that 'Bulwer's novels are decidedly superior to Sir Walter Scott's.' " Thus the *Microscope* in Louisville in 1824 looked to Sterne for precedent and reflected Addison and Goldsmith too. As for the more ambitious monthlies and quarterlies, chasteness and elegance were their long suits. Like their eastern models, they borrowed or stole in the name of culture. The *Western Review* (Lexington, 1819) had not only translations and imitations from Europe but poems in foreign tongues. The *Western Monthly Magazine* (Vandalia, 1830) planned to devote itself, in addition to statistics of Illinois, to essays, tales, "literary intelligence, fugitive poetry . . . . notices of the fine and useful arts." So did the *Hesperian*, the *Literary Focus*, the *Transylvanian;* and so, more futile than many another in the descending scale, did the *Rose of the Valley*. The exceptions, such as the *Western Monthly Review* and the *Illinois Monthly Magazine*, one of which tried to be local enough to deserve the attention of the future historian, and the other to make the West aware of itself, served only to mark the general rule. And the *Western Messenger*, which from 1835 on was the pre-eminent monthly, was the project of a number of Bostonians, many of them only temporary sojourners whose comings and goings reduced Cincinnati to an intellectual suburb of "The Hub," not a frontier town, and a near-frontier town only in physical location.

The story of the early fiction in the region is the same. Timothy Flint, the first novelist, wrote a great deal that was picturesque and exact about the region, but not in his novels. These, from one who knew his material as Flint did, were almost incredibly far-fetched and unreal. He evidently agreed with a strange dictum of Cooper that the new world was barren of material for the creative artist, on the assumption that the only source of such material was in the older civilizations. The tales of James Hall, mostly short stories, came a little nearer to reality. He intended, he said, to make fidelity the one claim for merit in his tales; they were to be of, by, and for the West. But he missed his mark when he made an old trapper exclaim at a critical moment, "Let us creep to yon log and rest our guns on it when we fire . . . . be cool—my dear young friend—be cool"; and he turned his back and shot in the opposite direction when he wrote of the scandalously riotous camp meetings. "So close is the union between good taste and religious feeling . . . . the mind elevated by the pursuit of a high object becomes enlarged and refined." There are realistic touches in the stories of both Flint and Hall, but in their romantic temper these men are far nearer to Rousseau and Cooper than to Rölvaag and Cather. With the notable exception of Mrs. Kirkland's *A New Home—Who'll Follow? or, Glimpses of Western Life* (1839), there was little before Eggleston's work of a generation later to mark the day of genuine realism in western fiction.

In his survey of the verse of the period Mr. Rusk once again did the work of the faithful historian without a thesis, but he provided the facts which show that the frontier was true to type in ignoring its frontier characteristics. There was a native tone to such songs and ballads as have survived orally, but in little else. Satire, as in the colonial near-frontier, but satire of the town and the townsman; a few passable lyrics to show that the love of beauty is never quite extinguishable; and epics! Let Dwight and Humphrey and Barlow share their doubtful honors with Genin and Emmons. Genin with his *Napolead* can easily cope with Dwight and Humphrey; and as for Emmons, his *Fredoniad: or, Independence Preserved, an Epic Poem on the Late War of 1812*, forty cantos in four volumes, can amply outweigh Barlow's *Vision of Columbus* of 1787 and the added *Columbiad* to which it was twenty years later expanded.

Finally, the characteristics of middle-western frontier stage and drama drive the point home. The seven thousand productions that Mr. Rusk pursued to their footlights were like any other seven thousand in the history of the American stage up to 1840. The English tradition was overwhelmingly predominant. Not only was the repertory not western —it was not even American; it was hardly up-to-date as played in America. It was incredibly close to the repertory of colonial days.

When in Cincinnati in 1801,

> The laughing muse here for the first time sate
> And kindly deign'd to cheer our infant state,

she did so in English idiom and mainly in the idiom of the eighteenth century. Anything further than this was in the fashion of New York, which itself was a reflection of later London modes.

The popular reading of the day was just as attentive to the East and to England. The appetite of Cincinnati and Lexington and Louisville was for dishes prepared in New York and London. There was a certain earnest protestation of interest in the high dignitaries of literature. Shakespeare was a name to conjure with, and Milton, and Pope The migratory New England Brahmins on the banks of the Ohio responded to Emerson's championship of Carlyle and spoke respectfully of Wordsworth and Coleridge and of Emerson himself. Cooper and Irving had no strong vogue, very likely because they had both experimented with western subject matter. The Americans dear to the hearts of the people who determined American bestsellers in the Ohio Valley were Fitz-Greene Halleck, James G. Percival, and Nathaniel Parker Willis. Percival was respectably ponderous; and Halleck and Willis were of the perennially popular type—nice, chatty magazinists with a gift for saying very little very pleasantly.

Of the English, the contemporaries whom everybody doted on were Mrs. Hemans, "L. E. L.," Miss Porter, Hannah More, and, of course, the twin giants of the day, Scott and Byron (only in the case of Dickens has the United States ever again been swept by such a reading epidemic), all of their works reviewed, most of them pirated, many of them parodied. They provided a background of common allusion, were variously dramatized on the western stage, and lent their names to the steamers plying the rivers—"Lady of the Lake," "Ellen Douglas," "Marmion," "Corsair," "Mazeppa," "Medora."

It is an immensely informative book, this of Mr. Rusk's on the literature of the middle western frontier; it shows what the frontier—or near-frontier—liked; and it shows that its more formal literature is the last of sources to look to for a realistic picture of what was going on there.

While the Rusk book was on the stocks, a scholar in Iowa was at work on a study of the frontier, specifically inspired by Professor Turner, and designed to include the forest, the prairies, the plains, the mountains, and the sea, after which detailed studies some "sound generalization" might be attempted. Miss Dondore's impressive book *The Prairie and the Making of Middle America* is accurately subtitled *Four Centuries of Description*, for the author is concerned with description, wherever derived, rather than with mere literature; and although she says in the Preface that "the problem is not so much one of finding the material as of eliminating it," the processes of exclusion seem to have been anything but ruthless. The early half of the volume is therefore drawn from accounts of the travelers and explorers, first French and Spanish, then English. This is within the professed scope of the book, but it offers the literary reader the choice of possessing his soul in patience or of skipping to the middle where the prairie begins to emerge in song and story.

From this point on, the findings about the prairie reinforce the findings about the Ohio Valley; all the early literature about it and most of the early writings done on the spot—if so vast a region may be so curtly alluded to—is pretty hifalutin stuff. Sentimentalism is the order of the day. The prairie itself is no more convincing than the conventional rural backdrop by a loft-painter who has never left the city. The love scenes are clumsily coy; the hero, if he is not an unmitigated prig, is the kind of bad man who is capable of every offense in the sight of man and God but who is redeemable at the mention of his grieving mother or the appearance of a defenseless and immaculate maid. The Saxon inclination to moralizing is given full license; observance of poetic justice makes the tales improving to the highest degree; and the style fits the substance in its stilted smugness. "On the whole, save for the one brief flowering in the work of Cooper, Paulding, and Simms, fumbling and inadequate without question was the novel's interpretation of the overflowing vitality, the emotional surge, the stirring adventures and grim endurance which with countless other diverse elements made up the developing life of the valley."

Through the Ohio Valley and out to the plains during the fifties and sixties something native at last developed in the shape of newspaper humor. It was journalistic because it could not find an outlet in any more elegant publications and because the newspaper public were its natural readers. It was deplored by gentlemen of letters like Edmund Clarence Stedman: "The whole country, owing to contagion of our American newspaper 'exchange' system, is flooded, deluged, swamped, beneath a muddy tide of slang, vulgarity, inartistic bathos, impertinence and buffoonery that is not wit." It was actually recorded by many a man of eastern birth: Artemus Ward, from Maine, who learned the West as a tramp printer; Petroleum Nasby, from New York, who edited country papers in Ohio; Josh Billings, of Massachusetts, deckhand, farmer, and auctioneer in Ohio; John Phoenix, of Massachusetts, western explorer and surveyor. It was Yankee humor applied to western men and manners. And even in book publication it was New York and Boston and Philadelphia that put the newspaper jocosities between covers and purveyed to an eager East the rough stuff of the West. Yet it was as western as Lincoln. Though its sober utterance of absurdity and its studied understatement were American rather than frontier in their quality, yet in its fondness for the tall story its humor partook of the breadth of the plains, where it still finds a natural soil.

In 1845 Col. Thorpe's *Big Bear of Arkansas* had a yarn of a farmer who planted his land to beets and potatoes and traveled for three months when he accidentally stumbled on a man who had looked over the place with an idea of buying him out. But the prospective purchaser was disappointed because the bottom land was full of cedar stumps and Indian mounds and could not be cleared. " 'Lord!' said I, 'them ar cedar stumps' is beets, and them ar 'Indian mounds' ar tater hills.' " There is a direct genealogy from this to

Archer Gilfillan's comments on Dakota weather in his *Sheep* of 1929: "Whatever the weather does in this part of the country, it does with intense and single-minded earnestness. The force, not to say violence of the wind may be judged by the fact that when it is due east or west the transcontinental trains frequently blow through our railroad towns as much as a day and a half ahead of schedule. When the country decides to go dry and stay dry—that is, in a strictly aqueous sense —the fishes have their choice of migrating down stream in their native element, or of sticking by the country and playing around in the dust for a while. When it decides to rain, the culverts come up out of the road for a look around and the bridges play tag with one another down the streams."

The volume on the prairie pursues the theme up to the present for the very good reason that one can find in its reaches both reminders and remainders of the frontier— matters which are reserved for later discussion. The Ohio Valley, in contrast, except for a few vestiges in the eastern mountain

counties, has entirely succumbed. It is settled and surrounded. The westering center of
population has long been crossing it. Its
chronicle is a closed chapter to which only
the superannuated can bring an active memory. As a frontier, it is a land of retrospects;
but the prairie still tempts one to forecasts;
comfortable middle-age can recall it as almost unpeopled, and it is yet open country
with mountain, plain, and desert beyond its
sunset line.

Miss Dondore, in her later chapters, points
to the fact that realism as to the prairie frontier gains with the years, though the persist-
ing romantic treatments are as meretricious
as ever; she acknowledges that the invading
cities increase the complexities of life in the
prairie regions; she speculates, in spite of
prefatory disinclination to generalize: "The
Valley's thought [and now, of course it is
the valley of the Mississippi and not the
Ohio] and the Valley's literature will always
be tinged by certain elements due to the
country, but it will probably be increasingly
conscious of the universality of human prob-

lems and emotions, increasingly conscientious about the manner of presentation.''

Yet, on the whole her presentation partakes largely of the characteristics of her material; the frontier not only does not seek to describe itself, it also fails to present its own epic implications. This book, inspired by Turner's thesis on the significance of the frontier in American history, contents itself with the visible matters of the frontier literature and leaves the significance unconsidered. Nowhere does it follow the most striking Turner observation—that the wilderness overcomes the individual pioneer, though the relentless and inexhaustible army of frontiersmen inevitably subdue the wilderness. A third book published in these years, 1925–27, amply compensates, however, for any timidities or restraints.

If Mrs. Hazard's *The Frontier in American Literature* had a subtitle, it might well be ''An Excursion in Criticism''; for Mrs. Hazard, in contrast with her two immediate predecessors, finds the concept of the frontier more interesting than the phenomena. She has read the gospel according to Turner and quotes the passage that excites every imaginative student. She becomes a hardy adventurer whom nothing can daunt or abash. Her frontiers are not merely geographical, nor of any other one kind. She reassures herself from R. T. Hill that the frontier means not only the frontier but all that has been frontier and all that has been affected by the frontier. Even this is not all, for the term is also protean and threefold: "It is the purpose of this study to trace in American literature reflections of the pioneering spirit; first on the frontier of regional pioneering, which is primarily concerned with man's attempt to control nature; second, on the frontier of industrial pioneering, which is primarily concerned with man's attempt to control the labor of his fellow-man; finally, on the frontier of spiritual pioneering, which is primarily concerned with man's attempt to control himself." If these free usages are sinful, she explains, the original guilt lies with

Turner and Paxson, historians. They are the serpents who tempted her in this historico-literary Eden.

Being thoroughly modern, she has not much use for the knowledge of good and evil as a possession of intrinsic value, nor much interest in Eden, except as a point of departure. Although it is her alleged business to make a map of the Garden and the outlying districts, her hand is on her holster as she peers through the transit—and she finds the hunting good. Whitman, though he thought himself a spiritual pioneer, "mistook the afterglow of the sunset for the glory of the dawn"; Simms wrote "in grandiose ambition which failed of realization"; Page did an album "of stiffly posed daguerreotypes"; Allen was "fanciful and tenuous." With conscious bravado Mrs. Hazard inquires if it is "too shocking a heresy to suggest that John Winthrop, Ralph Waldo Emerson, and George Follansbee Babbitt stand in logical succession?" It is no more shockingly heretical than it is shockingly unfair to suggest that when the gay excursionist arrives at the last chapter on *The Coming Age of Spiritual Pioneering*, she is sharing the same platform with Whitman and Emerson, rather to their tolerant amusement.

These historical commentaries on the literature of the early Middle West, the prairie, and the whole succession of frontiers are progressive and complementary. But when they appeared in close conjunction of time and subject, they reminded the reading public that a literary frontier boom was well launched and going strong. They derived from Turner, however, or shared with him, only his initial interest in the subject. The two more substantial books neither followed his interpretation nor substituted others of their own. They enrolled in the school of historians who content themselves with a careful recording of the facts, leaving to their readers some of the deductions I have noted. And they led to further applications of the frontier formula by scholars and critics and to its inclusion in a formal manifesto on *The Reinterpretation of American Literature*.

Since the publication of Paxson's *History*

of the Frontier and the literary studies of Rusk, Dondore, and Hazard, scores of books have appeared on the West, none of which is pure narrative or formal history and few of which were put forth as criticism. Taken as a whole, they are significant, however, not only as records but also as interpretations. And they are particularly interesting when read in the light of Turner's thesis as to the formative influence of pioneering. He asserted it in the initial essay, and he returned to it again and again:

"The wilderness masters the colonist." "In short at the frontier the environment is at first too strong for the man. He must accept the conditions which it furnishes or perish." "It took a century for this society to fit itself into the conditions of the whole province. Little by little nature pressed into her mold the plastic pioneer life." "European men, institutions and ideas were lodged in the American wilderness, and this great American West . . . . taught them a new way of looking at the destiny of the common man, trained them in adaptation to the con-

ditions of the New World." "American democracy was born of no theorist's dream.
. . . . It came out of the American forest,
and it gained strength each time it touched a
new frontier." The flood of recent non-fic-
tional books on the frontier may be viewed
with reference to the evidence it carries, or
fails to supply in confirmation of this line of
thought; and with reference also to the agree-
ment of the writers with Turner's belief that
the legacy from the frontier is a valuable
one.

It is safe to say that the less the writers of
these books were inclining to prove anything
the better they served as supporters of Turner's contention. For most of the authors
were world-weary and war-weary, turning to
the West to celebrate the passage of an heroic
age and applauding in that distant setting
men and events that could be duplicated in
every dramatic detail by the gangsters of the
nearest big city. Many of them were not recounting the achievements or the full experiences of the pioneers—little but their anarchy.
Most of them have enjoyed the fellowship of

kindred mind with Thomas Beer when, in 1926, they read a reminiscent passage in *The Mauve Decade:*

"The last Dalton slid across his brother's body. It was now ten minutes to ten. Sightseers poured from trains before noon and the corpses of Lord Tennyson's escort to Walhalla were photographed so that it could be proved that the Dalton gang was out of business after five years of graceful, even endearing performance. They were amiable and rather mannerly bandits, on the whole, and yet no ballad bears their name. The great tradition of Sturdevant, Murrel of the 'mystic clan' in Andrew Jackson's reign, Boone Helm, Billy the Kid and Jesse James ended here in an alley on the crackling sound of Carey Seaman's shotgun."

In this state of mind much has been written in the United States since the war. Across the Atlantic, Beverly Nichols, writing of *Sad Young Englishmen*, has described them as feeling that they are born only to suffer, that everything is futile, and that the best they can do is to harden their hearts. In 1924 some thirty Americans of like mind "symposed" a book on *Civilization in the United States*, starting from the assumptions that there was little but antithesis between preaching and practice in America, that it was by no means an Anglo-Saxon country, and that it was emotionally and aesthetically starved. The devotees of any thesis can find material for it almost anywhere if they look hard enough and interpret ingeniously enough. So the collaborators of *The Taming of the Frontier* are defenders of a thesis—that "the gods of individualism in both personal and community life have been thrown down to make way for the gods of standardization." They write as "serious defenders of vivacity and vitality in our national life," and they say that they have "good grounds for complaining to the police about the wanton cruelties inflicted by all this high pressure uniformity upon that unfortunate animal once called the American individual."

That is a fair warning. One turns in this book to the El Paso of early days, equipped with "blondes, bar-fixtures and building materials," and reads about the ominous arrival of a class of men who came with the intention of going into "more or less legitimate pursuits." By the time that they have fallen into the evil ways of shaving, bathing, wearing more than one suit of clothes and playing golf, the glory of the town has departed. One reads of Ogden that "since frontiers must fall, Ogden could not be Hell on Wheels forever"; one resorts to Denver, of whose early life it can be said that it was "vigorous if nothing else." So town after town has sunk into the slough of mediocrity and order and sanitation. Only the chronicler of Kansas City dares his colleagues: "It is with a fitting sense of shame that I here record the fact that Kansas City of today, Kiwanized, tamed, domesticated, Chamber-of-Commerced, Heart-of-America'ed as it is, with the issue of its civilization still in the balance, nevertheless to me is more desirable, more interesting in every way, than the bold, bad town that outfitted the Santa Fé and Oregon trade, the Pikes-Peak-or-Bust rush, and the cow country."

Middleton Murry, discussing "dissolution in literature," was writing specifically of England and the Continent when he recently declared that "a great part of the youth of the world is given over to an exaggerated cynicism," and that "there is no point of departure, no solid rock of social or religious security on which the present generation can begin to build. From the highest ability to the lowest it is infected by a desire for crude or refined sensationalism." He might have included an element in America in the indictment. The authors of *The Passing of the Frontier* find, not quite unanimously, grounds for their defeatist philosophy in the riotous anarchy of the frontier towns. With anarchy, their interest in the frontier ends. They turn to it in a repugnance for the present from which any escape is welcome. In a single phase of the frontier they find a melancholy satisfaction—a contemplation of the bad old days as they see fit to reconstruct them.

From these bad old days "Billy the Kid" stands out as the last great desperado—not the last to survive, for the death of Jim

Cummins, pal of the James boys, was recorded in the summer of 1929, and others still crop up from time to time, either as reformed and respectable or as pathetic down-and-outers. In Billy's short career from 1859 to 1880 he had a record of one man shot to death for each of his twenty-one years. He is the subject of two biographies, and he is recurrent in most of the chronicles of the cow country. The best account, by Walter Noble Burns, is a straight, unsentimental piece of narrative of unvarnished events. The author presents them starkly. Billy was an amiable, gentle, smiling, generously disposed, utterly ruthless murderer. When the story is finished, Old Man Foor takes the reader to the open spot where the town of Fort Sumner used to stand, and ruminates aloud: "I wouldn't say the kind of history he made entitles him to no monument, but it does seem to me that a fellow that raised as much hell as he did deserves some kind of a marker over his last resting place. It don't have to be a equestrian statue nor nothing big and fine. Just a little slab of gray granite would do."

And the author, standing there with Old Man Foor, admits that there is no need of artificial glamor to throw a rose glow over this "little cyclone of deadliness, whirling furiously, purposelessly, vainly between two eternities." For Mr. Burns, without resenting Billy, rather admiring the admirable in him, is willing to resign him to the past and to be reconciled to a social order that can express itself in something more constructive than homicide.

"Billy the Kid" met his death at the hands of sheriff Pat Garrett, not because he was a deadly gunman, but because he was a gunman in an evil cause. He was an outlaw, and that was bad; but he was "rustler," or cattle thief, and that was worse because it put him into active defiance of the code of the country as well as of the laws. The cattle country of today has lost its primitive qualities because of two homely inventions: barbed wire, with which an owner can inclose his stock, and windmills, by means of which he can water them. In the old days of open ranges and free grass, no man could keep track of his wandering property. Any large herd might include dozens or scores of brands. Collecting all one's own strays was impossible; returning them, impracticable. The consequence was that the dishonest had every inducement for large-scale thievery, and the honest built up a complicated system of marketing and accounting for each others' stock that depended on the highest type of organized fair play. The ranch owner was a kind of feudal lord over his domain, but his fortunes depended on an employee who was anything but a serf—"a proud rider, skilled, observant, alert, resourceful, unyielding, daring, punctilious in a code peculiar to his occupation, and faithful to his trust." The man who aspired to be a ranger must have all these traits or he must acquire them. This is what has made the chevalier of the plains the subject of so many thousands of pages of narrative.

He was a romantic figure, a creation of the circumstances with which he had to cope, one of the dynamic types who prefer to pay for their freedom with hardship, but of all these types—miners, trappers, sailors, explorers—probably the most peculiarly American. He has been the subject of a great deal of negligible fiction. Of late, too, he has supplied the matter for a lot of autobiographical volumes. As a rule he is better at spinning yarns than at making observations on life. Lee Sage, for example, the central figure of one of these books, *The Last Rustler*, says, "I believe the spirit of man builds the spirit of the country he lives in," and proceeds to a passage that proves the exact opposite. But John Young, leading character in another, *A Vaquero of the Cow Country*, states what most of the others reveal, in confirmation of Turner: "Hearing old-timers prate about their 'sacrifices' and trying to make martyrs out of themselves has always disgusted me. . . . . We were all pretty much creatures of circumstance. That circumstance sometimes brought out in us endurance and fidelity almost heroic . . . . but if we had not grown up with the soil between our toes, the wind in our faces, the starlight in our eyes, and a peculiar and strict code of ethics in our consciousnesses, we might not have been able to meet the tests that were applied."

The joint authors of *The Taming of the Frontier* look back upon it as to a lost estate—a state of primitive freedom never to be regained. The biographers and chroniclers of the cow country record a passing phase of civilization, and hold no thesis for it. A third point of view emerges from Mrs. Gerould's *The Aristocratic West*, a somewhat amusing attempt at interpretation. She is very eastern and very consciously magnanimous. In the Far West, she declares, there sprang up in pioneer days a more vital and romantic social code than any since colonial days. "We are very near to losing it, as we are losing the conditions that nurtured it, and the homogeneous, picked breed of men who created it. . . . . Yet by so much as it still shapes and colors the Far Western attitude to life is the Far Western attitude admirable, interesting, superior." She indorses the Grand Canyon, as it were, and pats the Rockies on the back.

To the easterner who has been away from

his old habitat long enough to sleep other-
wise than as a guest or a tourist, Mrs.
Gerould's determined magnanimity is quaintly amusing; and not because it is hers, but
because it is typically eastern. Having pene-
trated the continent west of Pittsburgh, she
is full of contempt for the provincials she has
left behind and for the traditions and prejudices with which their minds are packed.
She admits that there is no use arguing with
them, that western travel is their only possible cure; but she cannot resist trying to jolt
them out of their sectional pharisaism by
telling them some plain truths about the
superiorities of the people beyond the Mississippi Valley. She believes that the fine in-
tegrity of their characters is due not to any
results of their experience but solely to their
inheritance of the best from the colonial
East, and to the happy isolation which en-
abled them to preserve it uncontaminated.
They are courtly democrats, politically un-
important, as every presidential campaign
(up to 1924) proves to her. But they are
what they are because their immediate fore-

bears were endowed with certain basic virtues "liberally inherited, carefully cherished," and beyond question generously
bequeathed. These virtues were: courage un-
demanded in the East of today, honesty that
literally will not permit a thief or a lie to
survive, kindness that is willing to lay down
its life for a friend, and an attitude toward
women unequaled in the chronicles of chiv-
alry. This unequivocal code is ascribed by
Mrs. Gerould to the same people whom the
authors of *The Taming of the Frontier* looked
back on as cheerful blackguards and happy
bandits. To her the only West worth saving
is an orderly West which is being swept into
modern chaos. To them the only West worth
lamenting is a gay anarchy that is being subjected to modern standardization. In the
middle ground the writers who were not
struggling with a thesis show how the lion
of lawlessness and the lamb of courtliness lay
down together, and make no attempt to account for the twentieth-century West as a
progeny of their begetting.

It would be altogether misleading to imply

that in these fruitful three years of 1925–27
the American interest in the frontier, or surviving frontier traits was limited to historians, literary critics, social theorists and
their readers. Bill Hart and Tom Mix
reached a hundred through the film for every
one reached through print; Will Rogers came
into his own in these years; in these years the
rodeo was brought east, horrifying some of
the spectators, delighting others, but thrilling all. And a somewhat less than casual
glance at book and magazine publication for
the 1920's shows that there was a culmination of attention to all sorts of matters re-
lated to the men who were being "men in the
open spaces." The guides to books and mag-
azines tell the same story. Of collections
wholly or largely of frontier songs and ballads, there are six that one encounters in a
casual search. Four of them were published
in 1927. Of fourteen books on the cowboy,
three belong to 1926 and four to 1927. Paul
Bunyan, Munchausenized performer of prodi-
gies in the lumber camps, had his little vogue
from 1922 to 1925. Magazine articles on the

cowboy rose from an annual average of two from 1919 to 1921 to an average of nine from 1925 to 1927, and articles and stories of frontier life from three a year in the earlier period to twenty-four a year in the latter. One of the greatest moving-picture successes of these years was *The Covered Wagon*.

This whole frontier episode in literary history has been quite true to type. The frontier has been content to be itself, sing its songs, spin its yarns. It has never cared to put itself accurately on paper. The desire for realism about it has always been the desire of the remote observer. Now, however, all observers are remote at least in time, and most of us in mileage as well. As if to cap this modest climax, the newspaper of the day this was written contained a picture of Speaker Nicholas Longworth behind a cocked revolver apparently aimed at a bird's nest or a remote second-story window. It was a gun that had been owned by Jesse James and a present from a senator from Missouri. There you have the situation in a snapshot.

While the memories recede and the characteristics fade, the present is collecting them just as it collects ships' clocks or Windsor chairs. Naturally the most momentous record is in the pages of the novelists. All the foregoing has been no more than preliminary to them. All the rest of the story is theirs.

CHAPTER III

THE AMERICAN PIONEER
IN FICTION

✣

In the years after the World War, after the
first re-inventories of it and before the later
wave of renewed retrospection, America
looked westward—anywhere but at Europe
and, except for scandal, anywhere but at its
own political center. It followed Hudson to
South America, and O'Brien and Gaugin and
Maugham and Melville to the South Seas.
It looked backward as well as westward, as
we have been seeing, to the departed frontier;
but, as we shall see, less to historical or critical discussion than to fiction or other narrative. The time was ripe for men and
women who were versed in the life of the
pioneer and who could tell stories. And they
appeared.

These new writers were to write as from

the West. Nearly a hundred years before, Washington Irving had composed three volumes that were altogether foreign to his talents or interests. *A Tour on the Prairies*, he admitted, was recorded because the public expected it, though he felt no desire to write it and had no story to tell. For *Astoria* he had a little more of an inward impulse and far more of an outward one: John Jacob Astor furnished both documents and funds and supplied a dash of romance in his own career of immigrant boy turned merchant prince. But Irving rented his name when he accepted the subsidy of the millionaire and touched up the draft furnished by his nephew. Finally, *The Adventures of Captain Bonneville* was an aftermath of *Astoria* and another re-working of an original manuscript. All three books fail to catch the form and substance of the drama in the West. An appended paragraph to *Captain Bonneville* that alludes to "the romance of savage life" and laments the disappearance of "the gay, free trapper and his steed, decked out in wild array, and tinkling with bells and trinketry" betrays in its diction how the romance of Spain was being grafted on the epic of the plains. It is only less convincing than the concluding prophecy that the irreclaimable wilderness between the Rockies and the Sierras would one day "produce hybrid races like the mountain Tartars of the Caucasus" which would in time "become a scourge to the civilized frontiers on either side of the mountains." Steeds and cavalcades, Tartars and scourges, the whole concept was like the setting for a melodrama —*Metamora*, let us say, played by Forrest in a New York theater and viewed from seats supplied with the compliments of Mr. Astor.

Cooper, though prolific on the frontier and justly famous for his stories, wrote from a knowledge of the region rather than as a frontiersman. His father was a land-breaker incidentally to becoming a landlord. The son did not cling to his father's federalism, but he did not swing over to a feeling for the frontier as a melting-pot for the new democracy. Instead of thinking of it as the promised land in the westward sweep of civilization, he regarded it as the region from which

the Indian was being banished and where
such a pioneer as Natty Bumppo, hunter but
not settler, could find refuge from the oppres-
siveness of a congested society. His activities
are all on the wilderness side of the frontier
line. He embodies a philosophy of the town
that, coming from Greece, found lodging
among the English Deists, and joined in the
migration of ideas from the Old World to the
New. As a Deist and a frontiersman, he com-
bines the benevolence of the one and the
self-reliance of the other. The most dramatic
scene in *The Pioneers* represents this "nature's
nobleman" as reproaching Judge Templeton
(drawn from the elder Cooper) for invading
the rights of him who had ranged the woods
before the law had laid its hand on them. In
later novels Cooper bitterly deplored the for-
tune-hunting movement across the prairies
and the stay-at-home land speculators like
Irving. His frontiersman was a highly ro-
manticized figure, a solitary seeking escape
from the ways of the world, quite as much of
a poet and philosopher as a marksman and
woodsman, and endowed with all the virtues

of the nomad pioneer and with none of his defects.

Simms, significantly aware of the postfrontier settlement as a phase of frontier evolution, allowed a robustious, periwig-pated style to disguise the primitiveness of his theme. Eggleston, a stage nearer the present, knew his own already populated Middle West, and with a genuine realism created the frontier town with its narrow religiosity, primitive schooling, drab social life, shady politics, and shystering land speculation. So Irving dabbled with the frontier, Cooper fell short of faithful realism, Simms was an incorrigible melodramatist, and Eggleston stopped short of the retreating frontier, tarrying in the villages behind it. And the mid-century playwrights who resorted to the mid-western frontier for material did so only for comic types, which were most enjoyed by eastern audiences, while the Mississippi Valley was thrilling over *Richelieu* and *Virginius*, *Venice Preserved* and *Pizarro*, *The Iron Chest*, *A New Way To Pay Old Debts*, and the major tragedies of Shakespeare.

Mark Twain, out of his experiences in roughing it to the Coast, dealt more truthfully with his material. His picture of the claim-jumpers and prospectors in the mining regions is the record of a few fabulous strikes and a myriad of blasted hopes. And his summary of frontier evolution is mordantly ironic: "How solemn and beautiful is the thought that the earliest pioneer of civilization, the van-leader of civilization, is never the steamboat, never the railroad, never the newspapers, never the Sabbath School, never the missionary—but always whiskey! Such is the case. Look history over, and you will see. The missionary comes after the whiskey —I mean, he arrives after the whiskey has arrived. Next comes the poor immigrant with axe and hoe and rifle; next, the trader; next the miscellaneous rush; next the gambler, the desperado, the highwayman, and all their kindred in sin of both sexes; and next, the smart chap who has bought up an old grant that covers all the land; this brings in the lawyer tribe; the vigilance committee brings the undertaker. All these interests bring the newspaper; the newspaper starts up politics and a railroad; all hands turn to and build a church and a jail—and behold, civilization is established forever in the land."

There was need enough for this sort of writing to serve as antidote for the meretricious sentimentalities of Bret Harte, journalistic romancer from the East who turned the Coast pioneers into good copy for distant consumption: mining camps in which no one ever worked; mines that men sought for, found, and gambled with; miners who behaved like opera choruses; women freezing in snowdrifts with never a mention of the cold; Mother Shipton comfortably starving to death in ten days and departing life with an epigram; M'liss, shaggy as a Shetland colt, and sleek-souled as Little Eva. In fact, Bret Harte was only one of many contributors to an excessively conventionalized fiction of the Pacific Coast, much more stereotyped than Mark Twain's but far less so than Joaquin Miller's at his worst. All their western tales, and all of hundreds of others from or about the Far West were built, like a sham folk lore, from combinations of a few pat themes and *motifs* that soon were as outworn as the tritest poetic diction. They rang the changes on the miraculous reforms achieved by women and babies, the redeeming grace of loyalty between "pardners," the dramatic effect of recognition scenes between long-separated lovers. And they were ridden with type characters: the last man in the deserted camp, the learned recluse, the adopted Indian child or the white child adopted by Indians, the woman disguised as a man, the gallant gambler. Even the Plautine *miles gloriosus* was translated into the idiom of the mining camp.

On the whole, here, as farther east, the nineteenth century was true to the precedent early set for pioneer literature. The frontier, as long as it genuinely survived, was more interested in living than in contemplating life. The frontier, when it became the subject for literary treatment, was treated by visitors and sojourners and dressed for the market at that. Such a son of the West as Joaquin Miller, transgressing in prose, went to the most extraordinary excesses when he resorted to poetry. He knew better and emended himself in his later revisions, as with the sea-island Amazon who became the "Baroness of New York" but who, in her final literary appearance was not allowed to invade the metropolis and was made to behave like herself in her own habitat. Yet Miller's return to sanity of treatment partook partly of the nature of an artistic death-bed repentance and partly of a recognition that the frontier, now a retreating memory, was interesting enough in fact no longer to need the embellishments of false fiction.

The real frontier of the settler and homesteader, however, lay now between Eggleston's Ohio Valley and the Pacific Slope of Harte and Miller. Gold and silver regions seldom know the normal pioneer in normal conditions. Men invade, deface, strip, and abandon them. Their yield is only a medium of exchange; once despoiled, they are worthless. But the yield of the great valley and the high plains is food and raiment. Properly used, the value of these areas increases with the years, and on their expanses regular frontier evolution takes place. This evolution in the Mississippi Basin reached a stage in the 1890's where two factors were calculated to result in a literature of protest. One was that a wave of discontent at the plight of the agricultural class rose but failed to sweep the country first as populism and then as silver democracy; the other, that a second generation of westerners, free from the drive of pioneer life, and choosing the pen over the plow, used the novel to exploit the ills of the farmer. Two of the novelists who wrote in this vein near the turn of the century demand mention as last forerunners to the frontier expositors of the present.

Frank Norris, bred in California, schooled at Harvard, and stationed for a while in Chicago, projected in fine fervor an imaginative, semi-poetic "trilogy of the wheat." Of these novels, *The Octopus* assails the railroad combine which oppresses the helpless farmer and *The Pit* presents the symbol of the speculator who is equally regardless of producer and consumer. *The Wolf*, never completed, was to have dealt with the relief of an Old World famine. Norris aspired, like his own character, Presley the poet, "for the diapason, the great song which should embrace in itself a whole epoch, a complete era, the voice of an entire people." He conceived of an enormous, primitive force: "The Wheat that had killed Cressler, that had engulfed Jadwin's fortune and all but unseated reason itself; the Wheat that had intervened like a great torrent to drag her husband from her side and drown him in the roaring vortices of the Pit, had passed on, resistless, along its ordered and predetermined courses from West to East, like a vast Titanic flood, had passed, leaving Death and Ruin in its wake, but bearing Life and Prosperity to the crowded cities and centres of Europe." No one could attempt to divert this force to his own ends with impunity.

Norris' stories of the wheat are the combinations of hard fact and sentimental optimism that one becomes used to in the fiction of the frontier. He saw a situation through a farmer's eyes, and he aired the farmer's grievance against the corporation whose steel highway lay between him and his market. Norris' picture of the slaughter of a herd of sheep by an onrushing train through a cut in the hills implies that the railroad was not merely heartless, that it was deliberately malevolent. Yet he corrected this impression as belonging to the farmer and not to himself. To him the whole cruel story was only a phase in an epic process behind which lies essential righteousness. In an afterword he declared, "The larger view, always and through all shams, all wickedness, discovers the Truth that will, in the end, prevail, and all things, surely, inevitably, resistlessly, work together for good." It is a conviction that the author—one of the tender-minded of William James's classification—had a perfect right to hold. Being only an observer of the farmer's ills, he found it comparatively easy to hold this faith. His Pilgrim's pack of theology, economics, and art was a heavy one, and he was manfully but obviously staggering under it when he died with the trilogy still unfinished.

The Hamlin Garland of the nineties wrote in a different mood. He had learned the truth of pioneering days from harsh experience. He told his stories from the viewpoint of the women and children who had no choice but to follow the men and slave for them, and he was still full of a repugnance for the life that was climaxed in his escape to the East. So Garland pictured that life in *Main-Travelled Roads* and *Prairie Folks* with a fidelity that startled and offended both East and West— the West because it was grimly true, the East because it discredited a pleasant myth. In *A Member of the Third Estate* and *A Spoil of Office* he went on to present the hopelessness of the farmer as an economic and political catspaw, and in *Rose of Dutcher's Coolly* to show the aridity of life on the plains for a thirster after truth and beauty. Like many in his generation, Garland was much stirred by the social theses of Herbert Spencer and the economic theories of Henry George— they were major prophets for the young liberals; and for a while he was all aflame in behalf of his people. But he had never chosen the pioneer life; he did not feel committed to the land; and, as he stayed away, his ardor cooled and his vigor waned.

By the time he had finally turned from rural to urban life, the West to which he still reverted was become nothing but a backdrop for romantic drama just as Jack London's was for melodrama and Frank Norris' for problem plays. The choice did not turn out to be a profitable one. Apparently the public regarded the frontier as "old stuff" for the old-style, romantic approach, and was not ready for the new-style approach that he had just made and abandoned and was to resume a few years later. In the revival of interest in the frontier *A Son of the Middle Border* is a book to date from, but its date—1917—fairly raises the question as to whether it did not just miss the happy moment for a great popular success. The *Son* was greeted with respect, deserves it, and holds it; but this young man arrived at exactly the wrong moment. For the country was engrossed in the thought of two million other sons who were headed overseas. It could not be allured to turn westward and backward to one boy when it was agonizing over an army faced forward and eastward.

This book was a momentarily inspired return to the life from which Garland, as we shall later see, has correctly described himself as a "back trailer." Through the pathos of distance he captured the glamor of pioneering days, their restlessness, the grim tribute of grinding labor they exacted, the heart-rending sacrifices of the women who had no choice but to follow their men and slave for them, the unrewarded lives of the rank and file in the conquering pioneer hosts, the repugnance to it all that capped a boyhood on the Middle Border. This was what he had escaped from; but the first half of the book tells also of what, seen through his disillusioned eyes, lured and held the really incorrigible pioneers.

His father comes back from the Civil War with life to begin over again. The farm is his, for he made the last payment on a mortgage on the day of his enlistment. The elder Garland, like the McClintocks, his wife's family, is by nature enlisted in the conquest of the prairies, "clarion-voiced and tireless." They are like children, making a game of reaping, a race of husking, and a "bee" of threshing; and like children they are unstable and incurably restless for change. They sing a ballad in which the husband is irked because

> here I must labor each day in the field
> And the winter consumes all the summer doth yield,

but he gives way to the refrain of the wife:

> Oh, stay on your farm and you'll suffer no loss
> For the stone that keeps rolling will gather no moss.

The men prefer:

> Then o'er the hills in legions, boys,
> Fair freedom's star
> Points to the sunset regions, boys,
> Ha, ha, ha-ha!

It was the rallying song of the pioneer, "a directing force in the lives of at least three generations of my pioneering race." So for the Garlands it was from Wisconsin to Minnesota, from Minnesota to Iowa, from farm to village and back again, from Iowa to

Dakota; for the McClintocks no final repose till the Pacific stopped the western progress, for the elder Garlands none till they returned in poverty and defeat to Wisconsin.

To the young man who had gone East to educate himself, a visit after six years' absence threw a somber light over the whole picture. The glamor was gone. He saw that "the Song of Emigration had been, in effect, the hymn of fugitives." Nature was as alluring as ever in its beauties, but men and women had suffered in their struggle to possess an acreage and wrest a living from it. Every home he visited had its half-hidden evidence of striving and despair. Girls had wasted from beauty to premature old age. Shoulders were bent, and eyes were dimmed. Age had found no reward worth seeking, and youth was looking furtively or openly for avenues of escape. The whole enterprise of pioneering had been wasteful of energy and ruthlessly extravagant with life.

It is a notable book; but the author had to accept his reward in the form of election to the American Academy of Arts and Letters, small sales, and a royalty check that bought a new bath and a covered porch for his Adirondack cabin, though a little while before *Captain Stormfield's Visit to Heaven* had provided Mark Twain with an elaborate addition to an Italianesque villa. Which would be an altogether irrelevant comment if the subject of this meditation did not include popular response as well as artistic achievement.

In sober truthfulness about the prairie, author and public really came together in the 1920's with Herbert Quick's *Vandemark's Folly* and *The Hawkeye*. Quick had written attractive whimsies in the early years of the century, things that were neither sober nor true. While he was doing them, Frank Norris, thrilled with the responsibilities of the novelist, had propounded his poetized economic thesis, and William Allen White another with his *A Certain Rich Man*—both interesting documents, both chapters in the exploitation of the West, both just short of excellence as works of art, and both too early to profit from the rediscovery of the frontier.

Quick, however, had lived through the frontiering experience, surviving the hardships of the farm and the rough-and-tumble of politics. He had shared in the conquest of the open country, witnessed the tragic human sacrifice that is the cost of conquest, had fought the exploiters in behalf of his fellows, shouldered his way into leadership, through journalism had learned how to write, and at sixty was mellow, unembittered, sympathetic, ready for his crowning work. Events conspired for him as definitely as they had conspired against Garland so recently. The subject was ripe, and the public was ripe for it.

He wrote of the middle of the century in Iowa, not following the pioneers in their restless westward drifting, but staying with the settlers and growing along with them through two novels and a final volume of autobiography. What he told is authentic of home-finding, ground-breaking, town-building, developing into a matured community. There is no lack of hardship in the history This is supplied in abundance by gunmen, shysters, prairie fires, blizzards, droughts.

Yet withal it is a story of victory. The implication, granting viciousness in mankind and capriciousness, if not cruelty, in nature, is that life spares the deserving and punishes the wicked. Life had, in fact, dealt kindly with Herbert Quick, so kindly that he fell into the error of regarding his case as typical. That is the suggestion in the title he chose for his autobiography—*One Man's Life*. It contains a passage on meadow larks which reveals the optimistic bias of his theory of the westward movement: "I feel sure that I have heard the same individual bird change from the rather thin and tweedling song of the east to the bold and liquid sweetness of the west. . . . . My theory of the western meadow lark is that it is merely an eastern bird which learned in the great open spaces to give forth a broader and fuller message than that which it brought from the forests." It is a theory that springs from success which was gained and held in the new country. It is reinforced in the recollection that Harte and Clemens and Garland who returned to the East all showed an increasing tendency to "tweedle" in their later years. It is not born of ignorance—anything but that. Yet it could have been developed only by ignoring the grim experience of the majority, not so strong or so brave as this chronicler, who apparently was resolved to deal as kindly with life as life had dealt with him. Once more the soft heart of the novelist tempers the wind to the struggling plainsman.

There is a notable paucity, in both bulk and significance, of fiction that presents the native frontiersman in the first stages of pioneering—actually in contact with the earth. It remains for the chroniclers of the immigrant to do best with this phase; and we shall come to them. The American farmer was promptly carried by the novelists on into the Gilded Age, though it was not for him to enjoy its glitter; it was the drabbest of periods for the homesteader who had become the prairie townsman. There are plenty of reasons for this.

Life on the soil is elemental, positive, and exciting in its uncertainties. It demands knowledge and supplies it. It demands expertness and imparts it. Every operation has its technique; and every year, every month, offers its wide gamut of things to do. It is no accident of speech that the farm laborer is called the "handy man." He may be the man with the hoe for an hour or a half-day; but in the course of a season he uses fifty tools of a half-dozen kinds, from plow and scythe to paint brush and grindstone. The farmer's life, moreover, is a continual dealing in futures, from his winter planning and his spring borrowing to the shift from what he plans in the evening to what next morning's wind and weather dictate or permit. His life may be full of drudgery; but it is a life of crises too, with excitement in compensation for fatigue, with prospective results always in sight, and hope always over the horizon.

When either prosperity or failure brought a frontier farmer with such a schooling back into a prairie town, the odds were against him. With all his learning he had never learned to be a social creature. Caution in dealing with nature had grown side by side with suspicion in dealing with human nature; and it had bred a conservatism which made him equally leery of committing himself to a new farm machine, a new political doctrine, or a new interpretation of the book of Genesis. Relieved of the urgency of field and flock, he might substitute busyness for activity, but he was much more likely to subside into inertia.

It was not merely a move from too little human contact to too much: it was a transfer into a new order of civilization. On the soil in the last days of the last century he had been stubborn, resourceful, self-reliant. He had been endlessly industrious, but only primitively canny, for what he had regarded as his knowledge had been a strange blend of information, fallacy, and superstition. Rule of thumb had taught him much about planting, tilling, and harvesting; tradition had taught him as much more. He knew how to cut his potatoes for planting just as he knew that the best of crops would be blighted if they lay unsacked under a full moon. The ground-hog's shadow was no less certain in its prophecy for a season than a red sky at night for the coming day. He could not control the conditions under which he worked, and he could always lay a mishap to bad luck rather than to error.

The town he moved into had been invaded by applied science—not captured perhaps, but invaded and influenced by it. Machines turned out to be contrivances that can always be counted on if their conditions for working are met, and that are utterly uncompromising if the least of these are neglected. And the whole machine age, that builds and operates and finances the machine, turned out to be comparably methodical. Not only that, but though the same sort of method was coming to field and furrow, prosperity seemed to be reserved for the factory and to be withheld from the field. In the isolation of the farm the products of the factory had not seemed important; in the town they became all-important, and symbols of fortunes that were never piled up from the products of the farm.

All this served to thrust the retired farmer

back upon himself, offered him sterile hours of leisure in an alien world with nothing to do in them, nothing to interest him, no family habits of crafts or songs or games to resort to, these playing little part in the American countryside. He subsided all too naturally into such surroundings, filling the vacant hours with the swapping of yarns and gossip that has been dignified as cracker-box philosophy, and filling the once-open spaces with closed minds and a vague resentment at the revolution that an industrial age was hastening along. Ruth Suckow draws the portrait in August Kaetterhenry, one of her *Country People:*

"Emma said she believed half the trouble was that August had nothing to keep him busy any more. He did a little hauling. There was a job vacant in the lumber-yard. He would have liked to take it, at seventy dollars a month, but his old stubbornness kept him from it. He had said that he wanted to quit work. Actually he would have been glad at times to work on the roads or the section. But no work was vital any more.

No work looked forward to anything. He didn't want some one else for his boss. Everything that he had done had been for the farm. The farm had aways come first. He had always talked about retiring some day, quit this slaving; but he had never really looked forward to it. He had used every energy to build up the farm. He had done it, from almost nothing, by his own efforts, and now that he had made a fine place of it, Carl was living on it, and he had moved to town. Well, that was what everybody did. He would not have wanted to be like Herman, not able to do it."

Edgar W. Howe says that the vigilance of the gossip is the safeguard of morals in the town. To judge from his own epoch-marking *Story of a Country Town* and some thousands of pages of later testimony, he does too much honor to Mrs. Grundy's efficacy. Yet gossip holds a whip over the villager, inducing a guarded existence, bridling life with caution. The only note of general protest that has come out direct from this life shows

that the only articulate community consciousness in the broad region was the per-
ennial awareness, perennially justified in
America, that bank and factory were allied
against farm, and that the farm was the
hindmost, with the devil holding the mortgage—four billions worth in 1920. Though
the prairie states furnished occasional savage
critics of the economic order, and started
abortive, rival, self-defeating movements,
the natural fear of taking chances held them
in political line, and they floundered hope-
lessly in the attempt to find for themselves
any happy springs of enjoyment, any un-
drained sources of vital interest. For the ex-
frontiersmen of the prairie states, the evenings of their lives were like the evenings of
their days of labor: they were too tired to
feel, to think, and—most of all—to dream;
and the town to which they gave character,
though urban in the census report, was rural
in essential traits.

The worst human fruits of such an era are
to be found in the first half of *Spoon River*

Anthology; the average, in *Main Street;* E. W. Howe is one of the best. In his *Plain People* he has reprinted with evident satisfaction Mr. Mencken's statement of the sum of his philosophy: "One day, seeking to introduce him to the readers of a magazine, I tried to put his general point of view into half a dozen plain propositions. This is what it came to:

"1. The only real human motive is intelligent self-interest; altruism is not only bogus, but impossible.

"2. The first object of self-interest is to survive. The possession of money makes it easier to survive. Ergo, it is virtuous to get money.

"3. A man who gets it is a better citizen than one who doesn't; what he does for himself also benefits the community in general.

"4. The aim of all reformers is to get something for themselves. They pretend that it isn't; hence, even when they chance to serve good causes, they are liars.

"5. Any American of average talents and decent industry can get enough money, barring acts of God, to make himself comfortable.

"6. Any man who fails to do so shows an unfitness to survive, and deserves to be exploited by his betters.

"7. The people have a remedy for all public abuses in their hands. If they fail to get relief, then the blame lies wholly upon their own credulity, emotionalism and imbecility."

If Mr. Mencken and Mr. Howe had not regarded this as a fair statement, the one would not have made it nor the other have quoted it. Yet from any unsympathetic critic of Mr. Howe it would stand as more of an indictment than an indorsement. It is the law of the jungle; it disregards even the small subscription to religion or to "moral perfection" conceded by Benjamin Franklin, and the merciful doctrine of moral imperfection propounded by Clarence Darrow; it shows all the deference for vested property inherent in the Constitution before the addition of the Bill of Rights; and at half a dozen points the "plain propositions" are in conflict with each other. Yet even in its self-contradictions it doubtless is a fair statement of Mr. Howe's philosophy, and a partial statement of the views of the postfrontier for which he was so long an eminent spokesman.

Thus spake Atchison, Kansas; but Emporia, Kansas, made reply, William Allen White, tender-minded and more cosmopolitan, retorting to "Ed." Howe, the tough-minded provincial. On five of the seven theses laid down by Mr. Mencken they disagree. A reference back to this list, and a comparison by numbers, will give the whole story. White's convictions can be cited by chapter and text from *The Editor and His People:*

1. Human nature is steadily changing from a belief in untrammeled self-interest to the practice of altruism.

2. Self-interest leads to demands for special privilege and to viciously unscrupulous corporate practices.

3. Vicious corporate practices are good neither for the people who gain nor the people who lose by them.

4. It is through the activities of cranks and reformers that the people are taught social wisdom. These leaders fight in season and out of season for the people.

6. There are many incapable and irresponsible people in the world who are more sinned against than sinning. They deserve mercy as well as justice.

On two points only do the eminent Kansans agree: (5) that the man of average talents and industry can make a decent living, and (7) that the voice of the people is anything but the voice of God, and credulity and emotionalism are still the lead-horses attached to the American bandwagon.

Both men speak, perhaps, for Kansas, but as from watch towers. "Ed" Howe is old enough to be reminiscent of frontier days. He recalls Indian fights, and buffalo hunts, and the last of the Jameses, the reign of fanatical orthodoxy, anti-slavery agitation and the Civil War, the coming of the railroads, land speculation, financial wild-catting, scurrilous newspaper feuds. Then—with the changing of the town from the eastern outpost of the cattle trails to the western goal of the barnstormer—the coming of Beecher and Ingersoll, Oscar Wilde, Fannie Davenport, and Minnie Hauk—worldliness sets in. His wedding "had in it a simulation of the grandeur of palaces, courts and cathedrals, although it occurred in a story-and-a-half house in a country town"; and he finally achieves for himself a residence with steam heat and "the best bed-room in Kansas, with a private bath," though he tries to compensate for the palatial grandeur by calling his estate "Potato Hill." Howe's chronicle is a recital of all sorts of facts and opinions tinged by a latent sentimentalism reeling helpless in the face of overwhelming fact; in the language of the prize ring, not "down and out," but "out on its feet." He favors the doctrine of predestination "somewhat liberalized"; but he believes that the people who have gone wrong ought to have behaved. And always this modernized Franklin of the prairie couples industry and thrift with good behavior and success.

William Allen White is less static a character. His selection of editorial articles contains a section headed "The Decay of a Conservative"; a semi-centennial article on Emporia traces his growth from dreamy romanticism over a town that existed only in legend to a recognition of the town in fact; but he does not allege that the town has kept pace with him. The Emporia of *In Our Town* is Sweet Auburn, Cranford, Old Chester, Friendship Village. There is no evidence that in the general consciousness it has participated in any epic movement, that it is the heir of any heroic age. He describes Kansas as fair and fat with prosperity; and yet, mysteriously, "Kansas is the Mother Shipton, the Madame Thebes, the Witch of Endor, and the low barometer of the nation. When anything is going to happen in this country, it happens first in Kansas. Abolition, Prohibition, Populism, the Bull Moose, the exit of the roller towel, the appearance of the bank guarantee, the blue sky law, the adjudication of industrial dispute as distinguished from the arbitration of industrial differences—these things came popping out of Kansas like bats out of hell. Sooner or later other states take up these things, and then Kansas goes on breeding other troubles. Why, no one seems to know."

The springs of abolition and prohibition were in New England Puritanism. The issues were moralistic; the will to power, the desire to dictate, and the fighting spirit have a clear genealogy through Plymouth and Massachusetts Bay by way of the English Commonwealth to the Reformation. The springs of populism and progressivism were in the West, in a vague discontent; but the will to power and the fighting spirit were lacking. The low barometer is not the cause of anything, it is only the indication of a symptom. The old frontier is become a seat of infection rather than a seat of power. It has just enough recurrent energy to send occasional scattered "insurgents" to Congress, but not enough courage or solidarity to rally and enlist in their support.

In his interpretation of the Mississippi Valley ex-frontier, Sinclair Lewis leads the

way in critical sagacity. *Main Street* sets its
key with the opening strain of a rebellious
girl who is the spirit of the bewildered Middle West looking out over the country from
a Minnesota hillside recently crossed by Indians and fur-traders. She is a student in a
sectarian college, eager to know and to live,
unaware of the world's capacity for dulness
or its gift for casual cruelty. She has been
brought up in a Minnesota New England
town which has a firmer anchorage in the
past than most of the surrounding communities. She wonders whether its people feel free
to challenge the "sanctified lies" and the
"ancient stale inequalities."

When, after her marriage, she moves to
Gopher Prairie, she discovers that her new
neighbors do not know what conversation is,
and that they have lost the power for im-
personal thought, and, worse still, the mood
for spontaneous play. She finds that the early
autocracy of Yankee professional men has
passed to the merchants, but the tribal rulers
of the town are so vigilantly watched that in
their observance of the accepted morals and

accepted chicaneries they have become hypocrites to the core. She is told that the spirit of the place is sound, wholesome, but afraid. She observes that it gives vocal subscription to sweetness and not too much light, that the best citizens are as solicitous for their pocketbooks as they are for their reputations. In short, except for freedom from an established squirearchy, Gopher Prairie is like all villages in all countries that have "lost the smell of the soil and have not gained the scent of patchouli." She discovers that only in the awful and limitless surrounding plains does she find dignity and greatness. Some invisible barrier excludes these qualities from the town. It has its own credo:

"The Baptist Church is the perfect, the divinely ordained standard in music, oratory, philanthropy and ethics.

"The Republican Party, the Grand Old Party of Blaine and McKinley, is the agent of the Lord and of the Baptist Church in temporal affairs.

"All socialists ought to be hanged. . . . .

"People who make more than ten thousand a year or less than eight hundred are wicked.

"Europeans are still wickeder.

"It doesn't hurt any one to drink a glass of beer on a warm day, but anybody who touches wine is headed straight for hell. . . . .

"The farmers want too much for their wheat.

"The owners of the elevator-companies expect too much for the salaries they pay.

"There would be no more trouble or discontent in the world if everybody worked as hard as Pa did when he cleared our first farm."

The defenders of this orthodoxy look with fear and suspicion on any who either inquire into these theses, disregard them, or look beyond them. Carol Kennicott finally succumbs to them, for she is only the averagely courageous and energetic idealist.

Gopher Prairie multiplied by a hundred becomes the middle-western metropolis of Zenith. According to Lewis, the difference between the two is only quantitative. But the mere mass of the bigger-scale community is less resistible by the average. George F. Babbitt has probably less of initiative than Carol started with. His fight is less open or prolonged, so much less so that it is hardly a fight at all, and could be disguised like an official report of a military retreat as successive assumptions of more strategic positions. And his tactics are cautiously military, too, in being always pursued with primary attention to the base of supplies. Yet, until he is overwhelmed, Babbitt dreams and yearns. Even when he has married the wife he had not aspired to, and thriven in the business he did not elect, he distrusts the hullaballoo of busyness in which he is involved. He has secret leanings for Seneca Doane, the radical lawyer, and knows in his heart that Doane is right in his contempt for good, clean, domestically sound, throat-cutting pirates who shout good fellowship and hesitate at nothing that stands in the way of success. He slips away to a vacation far from the crowd to think things over, but is pulled back so completely into the maelstrom that he becomes a minor prophet for the gospel of efficiency and a dispenser of ominous threats to the un-American skeptics who ask how the ship of state became transformed into a national bandwagon and want to know where it is going as it thunders past them along Prosperity Boulevard. Yet the solidest satisfaction he gains in the whole story is in the fact that his boy has the combined impudence and recklessness to have a mind of his own and go his own gait.

The theme of *Main Street* and *Babbitt* becomes the thesis of *Arrowsmith* and *Elmer Gantry:* that the atmosphere of the Middle West is asphyxiating to the scientist but elixir for the charlatan and demagogue. As documents, these two books are significant. They confirm Howe and White. They have been impressively confirmed by the careers of Billy Sunday and W. J. Bryan. As stories, they are in a trough between the wave-peaks of *Main Street* and *Dodsworth*—but *Dodsworth* we must postpone to the very end of our chronicle.

CHAPTER IV

THE IMMIGRANT PIONEER
IN FICTION

⚜

THE immigrant pioneer and his treatment
in American fiction have been reserved for
this place only because the best novels on the
subject have appeared so lately. As far as
either sequence or consequence prevails between frontiering and its literary fruits, the
order is always from the temporary visitor,
like John Smith or Bret Harte (sole likeness
to conjoin them), to the permanent sojourner, like John Cotton or Joaquin Miller,
to the native-born, like Cotton Mather and
"Ed" Howe, and finally to the back-trailers,
like Benjamin West and Hamlin Garland.

From the outset the immigrant has been
communicative, but for generations most of
his writing about the frontier was in letters

or official reports. It was not until well into the eighteenth century that anyone undertook to theorize notably on the subject or to look westward beyond the visible horizon. When they did—when such a man as the author of *Letters from an American Farmer* wrote on themes like the nature of the American or the perils of the frontier—the result was what we recognize now as the conventional compound of sober fact and sentimental theory. As for the theory, Crèvecoeur had a pretty one; and he dressed it up eloquently: "What, then, is the American, this new man? He is either an European, or the descendant of an European, hence that strange mixture of blood which you will find in no other country. I could point out to you a family whose grandfather was an Englishman, whose wife was Dutch, whose son married a French woman, and whose present four sons have now four wives of different nations. *He* is an American, who, leaving behind him all his ancient prejudices and manners, receives new ones from the new mode of life he has embraced, the new government he

was shameless and hideous. They were a forlorn hope, a vanguard ten or a dozen years ahead of the main army. They would perform the first heavy labor and then either gravitate up to prosperity or be pushed out by their successors into a new front-line of semi-savagery. "Such is our progress, such is the march of the Europeans toward the interior parts of this continent. In all societies there are off-casts; this impure part serves as our precursors or pioneers." Theory begins to run away with him until he remembers that his father was a pioneer. But it is a hypothetical father, for his own never came to America; and he salvages the imaginary one by making him an honest and respectable exception.

It is just as well, then, in approaching the recency of fiction about the non-English-speaking immigrant in America, to remember that the recency is in the fiction and not in the subject. Place-names make a palimpsest of the American map: Indian names everywhere on the original parchment; English names on the eastern seaboard from

York Village to Yorktown and beyond; village names for the commoners in the north—Plymouth and Greenwich and Chester and Dover; royal names for the cavaliers of the south—Georgetown and Charleston, Virginia and the Carolinas; fond reminiscent names—New Hampshire and New London and New Jersey. New Rochelle, too and not far away Havre de Grace, though one looks for most of the French names in an encircling zone from Detroit and Marquette and La Salle to St. Louis and Louisiana and New Orleans. Spanish names beyond these from San Antonio to La Jolla and from Los Angeles to San Francisco. And all between, names from every part of the British empire, from all over Europe, from the Orient, with corruptions that only the philologian can trace and inventions that only the unbridled imagination could have contrived. The last four teams to survive in a national interscholastic contest of 1930 represented public schools in an Athens, a Jena, a Corinth, and a military academy named after St. John.

This is nothing to exclaim over; it is

simply something to recall in a country whose Columbus mustered on shipboard, besides his Spaniards, an Irishman, an Englishman and a Jew, and whose original Atlantic colonies were peopled by Dutch and Swedes and two hundred thousand Germans, who might have looked westward had they known what to look for, beyond a zone of seventy thousand French to a host of Spaniards in the Southwest who may have outnumbered the English and probably could have outbid them in an open auction of the intervening territory. Just as it is also something to recall in this Saxon-dominated country of the twentieth century, that 1848 sent over fresh hundreds of thousands of Irish and Germans, and that from 1860 to 1890 Norway gave the United States a fifth of its population. The emphasis given to immigration with the fresh influx and the change of origins in the nineties, together with the cramping of the western outlet, made the oldest fact in white American history—its composite nature—take on the semblance of a new one. Even in the earlier literature, there is a substantial body of fiction partly buried in the forgotten past and partly hidden in the foreign languages in which it was composed for foreign-born Americans and their European friends.

Much of this narrative is by sojourners rather than settlers, was written to sell, and was tinctured as usual, whether through misconception or sheer guile, with the strongest flavors of romantic unreality. The archetype is Gilbert Imlay's *The Emigrants* of 1793. It is a book with a thesis: that England is politically corrupt and that American innocence is bliss. Every character, says the author, is drawn from a model; but every one of them can be found in the pages of Frances Burney. These people, the best of them ruined in fortune and forced "to seek an asylum in America," find the asylum rather turbulent; but after a rough experience crossing the Alleghenies and following the Ohio as far as Louisville, encountering the grandeurs of nature and the magnanimities of the noble red man, the heroine "perfects her prospect of happiness," and the hero's understanding has not only been regenerated but his person has already become so robust that he has now more "the appearance of an Ancient Briton" than of the London dandy of the opening chapters. Imlay has performed the office of a moral instructor.

Gustave Aimard, Frenchman, entertained, perhaps, an equally high purpose, but wrote pattern blood-and-thunder tales with all the conventions of Chateaubriand and all the devices of the Beadle dime novels. And his total irresponsibility about the simple facts almost rivals Munchausen's. Though the Germans are, as one would assume, a shade more scrupulous, Mollhausen was too prolific to be careful in any respect, Gerstacker was fascinated with what today is dignified as "organized crime" and did well by it in its border manifestations, and Sealsfield (Karl Postl) leaned to the poetic pictures of nature and deserved Longfellow's commendation for this feature of his writing.

But enough of the earlier writers. Two of the three stories in Gertrude Stein's *Three*

Lives, her first book (1909), give promise of much. But her return in the ponderous *The Making of Americans* (1926) is beclouded by the increasing stylism that was to reduce her later works to hardly more than studies in eccentricity. When we turn to the present movement, we find that Willa Cather's three pre-eminent books—*O Pioneers*, *The Song of the Lark*, and *My Antonia*—come far closer to the theme of the alien immigrant on American soil than anything that preceded them. The stories of Alexandra Bergson, Thea Kronberg, and Antonia Shimerda are about the newly transplanted European. In them, and particularly in the first and last, are the prairie farm and the prairie town. They are chronicles of hard, dreary beginnings and ultimate success, the development of a new social order, the assimilation and amalgamation of Swedes, Czechs, and French, "passionate souls, expiating their mistakes in bewildered pain." In the first of the stories looms the splendid figure of Alexandra, masterful, too magnanimous to be understood, doomed to spiritual solitude among her own

people, but indomitable. Through the gentle
melancholy of the closing lines glows an im-
mortal strength. In the second appears Thea,
equally single-minded and equally poised,
who succeeds on the stage as Alexandra succeeds on the plains. Through the two Miss
Cather identifies the spirit of the pioneer
with the spirit of the creative artist, ignoring
all the lesser figures in the epic of the frontier, just as she ignores orchestra, chorus,
and stage hands in the triumph of the opera
singer. But from the last of the three stories
emerges Antonia, apotheosis of the pioneer
working-woman, Martha glorified on the
frontier, a rich flood of life, suffused at the
end in a sunset gleam against the background
of field and furrow.

Yet Miss Cather makes an approach to the
final treatment of the non-English-speaking
immigrant of the plains, and not an arrival at
it for a definite reason, a reason that divides
itself into two: She is a Nebrasko-Virginian
writing of immigrant folk. That means, for
one thing that she knows her people only as
well as they can be known through sym-

pathetic observation. They are idealized, interpreted as creative personalities, vested with the characteristics of the creative artist whom Miss Cather knows by nature as well as from observation. And it means, for another thing, that, since she knows her immigrants through sympathetic observation, when sympathy and observation fall into conflict, sympathy triumphs. She has the kindliness of an indulgent literary parent; she is unwilling to resign them to their fates. She does not, therefore, record the conquest of the individual pioneer as the pioneer army conquers the plain, though she allows her fictive offspring to stray into the very last ditches of near-defeat before she serves as counterleader of valiant relief parties in a series of incredible rescues.

What she lacks, or lacked, for she has abandoned this field, was the hardihood to submit to her material. For complete fidelity of portrayal there are needed scrupulous realism, the conscientious exactitude of the expert court witness, and an unwavering desire to follow the implications of the testimony wherever they may lead. "The more such an author," writes Glenway Wescott in one of his prefatory passages, "has in common with his characters, the better; typical trivialities surpass in significance the noblest feelings; an immediate report is more valuable than reminiscences, the rest is lyricism. . . . . No judicious novelist . . . . will strive to outdistance life; he will choose problems which only *seem* insoluble, which in some corner of society, in some small illustrative scale, have been solved. The future of America is a genuine riddle. The riddle of a sphinx with the perfect face of a movie star, with the dead-leaf complexion which is the result of this climate, our heating system, our habits." The passage is completely pertinent to what remains in the present chapter, for it leads to an author who has all in common with his characters; and it proceeds to his trilogy, still uncompleted but headed for a third generation, grandchildren of immigrant stock and merged in a civilization which popularly idealizes the face of the sphinx, be it Buster Keaton's, Bill Hart's, or

Calvin Coolidge's. Wescott's passage might have been written explicitly about the Norwegian-American, Ole Edvart Rölvaag.

The Norwegian migration seems to have been the last considerable one to sweep out over the western lands. It was not until after the Civil War that the Scandinavians made their way into North Dakota, where they now mount up to a third of the population. At the last census more than a million born in Norway or of Norwegian parentage lived in the six north-central states. And, as three-fourths of these have followed rural lives, they have been peculiarly free to foster the language and traditions of the homeland. Harsh circumstances forced them to take bodily leave of the old country. They were grateful and hopeful in the New World, but their hearts were still in Norway. And as they are a literate people, they became prolific in authorship, publishing in their own tongue for their own people on both sides of the Atlantic. Two of the names most often associated with their migration do not really belong to it: Johann Bojer, because he has been a European observer; and H. H. Boyesen, because in his American career he did not elect to cast in his lot with the immigrants, joining the eastern professoriate and writing in English.

But there have been scores upon scores of journalists, hundreds of contributors to poets' corners—little corners of sentimental Norway tucked off in corners of the Northwest—and a smaller but more important number of travel-writers and novelists. Prevailing in their writings is the consciousness of the pilgrim and the sojourner. Often the title-page reveals that the literary waif was privately printed; in Iowa City, in Ephraim, Wisconsin, in Watford City, North Dakota. Other books were issued from Norwegian presses: the Amundsen Publishing Company, Decorah, Iowa; the Augsburg Publishing House, Minneapolis; the International Press or the Heiborg Printing House, in New York and Brooklyn; or with Aschehoug and Company, Oslo. Almost without exception the two lands are linked together in the stories:

a poor boy comes to America, thrives, and returns to claim his sweetheart and wreak vengeance on a Norwegian oppressor; a poor boy comes to America, sends for his sweetheart, and reaches the high goal of the pulpit; a poor boy comes to America and has a daughter who rebels at the sordidness of Jonasville, another Gopher Prairie, and goes to Chicago where she marries one Miles Standish Ward; a poor boy comes to America and makes his fortune but sinks into spiritual bankruptcy; another develops into solid, courageous citizenship, bent on contributing the best of Norwegian character to the land of his adoption; a Norwegian sculptor strives to find his place in the American scene.

To this tide of fiction from O. A. Buslett, Peer Stromme, Waldemar Ager, Simon Johnson, and H. A. Foss, Ole Edvart Rölvaag had been contributing with his *Letters from America*, *The Forgotten Path*, *Two Fools*, *The Ship of Longing*. But to name them so is misleading, for, like all the others, they had been published in Norwegian, and in his case, only in the United States. Then came throughout the reading-world a new vogue for the novel of the soil, accelerated by Hamsun's influence; then also in the United States, a fresh zest for frontier tales; and then, finally, the announcement that Bojer was planning to treat the theme of the Norwegian immigrant on the American frontier. It was an unconscious challenge to Rölvaag which he at once accepted. In 1924, within a month of each other, the two novelists published. In 1927 *Giants in the Earth* was issued in an English version which within a twelvemonth ran to forty-four printings. *Peder Victorious* followed two years later; a third volume is in process; and the apparent interruption of the trilogy with *Pure Gold* is only apparent, for this is the English version of *To Tullinger* (*Two Fools*), a story of 1920.

An exceptional man, Rölvaag affords exceptions to two broad generalizations about frontier life and frontier literature without overthrowing either of them. According to Turner's "law," the wilderness masters the colonist and transforms him into a new,

American product. It has done so with Rölvaag, but has left him an exception to the
rule by mastering him without overwhelming him. Again it is the usual case in frontier
evolution that when the pioneer becomes
articulate he writes literature for the frontier
but not about it, or if he writes about it he
converts it into a circus or a masquerade or a
sentimental drama. But Rölvaag has com-
pressed great breadth and variety of experience into a single career; not content with
mastering two languages and blending two
cultures, he has progressed from the life of
the toiler to the life of the scholar and thence
to the life of the artist. He is what Nathaniel
Bumppo Cooper might have been, or Antonia
Shimerda Cather, if such characters had ever
lived and written. He has not only seen all
that he has written about; it has all been in
the warp of his emotional experience. When
he writes, therefore, he is not the frontiersman trying to handle a pen with his trigger
finger, or a Joaquin Miller in sombrero and
boots at a London *salon*. He is the only kind
of novelist that could vie with Johann Bojer

and surpass him, for he is the primitive subject of Bojer's *The Emigrants* and he is also
Bojer's peer as a creative writer. The almost
simultaneous appearance of *Giants in the
Earth* and *The Emigrants* is not the unaccountable coincidence that it seemed, though the
story is important here chiefly as it affects
Rölvaag.

The fundamental difference in the ap-
proaches of Bojer and Rölvaag is apparent at
a glance. Bojer writes as a Norwegian about
emigrants; Rölvaag, as an American about
immigrants. Rölvaag has lived what Bojer
has heard about even more remotely than
Miss Cather did. Bojer makes a leisurely
start with Morten Kvidal in Dyrendal and
returns there with him in the concluding
pages. He is a Norwegian author, aware of
the lure of the Northwest for multitudes of
his countrymen, interested enough in it to
have posted himself on the essential facts.
But to the end his attitude toward his material is that of the home-stayer who listens
with fascinated attention to the tales of the
returned traveler. It is all very extraordi-

nary, he seems to say: the voyage, the last slow journey over the prairies, the locating of the claim, the breaking of the ground, the raising of the first crops, the numbing experiences of heat and cold, of pests and fires, and withal the steady progress toward freedom and fortune. He is so absorbed in a thousand unfamiliar events and circumstances that he feels

> no need of a remoter charm,
> By thought supplied, nor any interest
> Unborrowed from the eye.

Only in the closing paragraphs does he convey the idea that there are epic implications in all this.

In contrast, Rölvaag's participation in the experience gives to his treatment of the same theme an emotional depth that could not be expected from a mere observer. The narrative undertaking to which he set himself is the one so often essayed by his Norwegian fellow-immigrants: to present through event and circumstance in the new land the double ordeal of the alien of another country and of another speech. He must not only break the kinship of the soul and the soil in which it has grown (the pioneer from the eastern states or from the British Isles has done that); he must cope with a new language. Yet genuinely to acquire a new speech demands "a spiritual readjustment which is forever beyond the power of the average man because it requires a remaking of soul. He cannot give up the old, because that would mean death to him, and he cannot master the new—the process is simply beyond his powers." This is a phase of national assimilation that any American, or any Norwegian, can grasp intellectually; but only the Norwegian-American who has survived the struggle can grasp and present its emotional verity. The physical conquest of a wilderness does not leave the immigrant time or energy for language study, and acquiring a language means much more than the routine task of building up a workaday vocabulary. The complete transition from one land to another can come only with so intimate a mastery of the new language that the emotional life can find spontaneous outlet through the new medium. And that is the miracle of acquiring a new soul that only one in ten thousand may achieve.

It is the tragedy inherent in this situation that leads to the conquest of the pioneer—to Turner's brief statement that the wilderness masters the colonist. The immigrant pioneer is confronted by peril on peril: first, of physical defeat while he and his kind are transforming the surface of the earth; then, as the community closes around him, of social submergence without inner adjustment; finally, if he have the capacity for making a new soul, which is forever beyond the power of the average, of the ostracism that follows independence or the surrender to Mammon that follows material success in the midst of small-town Philistinism. One can trace the befalling of these catastrophes on the chief figures in the Rölvaag chronicle.

Taking *Giants in the Earth* and *Peder Victorious* as portions of a single long narrative, the natural division falls, not between the covers of the two books, but in the middle of

the first volume with the end of the part
called "The Land Taking." This is a tale of
primitive life that can be considered wholly
in folk terms. Per Hansa, the hero, is the incarnation of primitive strength. He builds
largest, plows longest, sows earliest, laughs
loudest, rages most wildly, forgives most
quickly. He is pre-eminent in all performance. His wife, Beret, is primitive fear.
Her man has overwhelmed her in love and
marriage. She is in perpetual terror of pun-
ishment for her surrender before wedlock,
harassed by the thought of unfaith to the
land she has abandoned, saddled with all the
burdens of both Christian and pagan superstition. Most of all, the prairie overwhelms
her in its vast reach and ominous silence. In
this folk story the prairie itself is primitive
nature, the earth-spirit as familiar to a people who have always had to contend with
it—no South-European Ceres. So the primitive hero confronts the plains. "From eter-
nity the prairie had lain here, lapping sun
and drinking moisture, and had peered up
into an endless blue day, brimful to running

over. At evening it had listened to strange tales told by the twilight breeze. But now other concerns had come to occupy the thoughts of the Great Plain, giving it not so much as a moment of rest. The sod huts crumbled and merged again with the earth out of which they had come. Sod is but sod, after all, and was never meant to shelter human beings so long as they can stand on their legs. . . . . Large dwellings and huge barns sprang up all over. Summers the Great Plain tried tornadoes; in spring and autumn, prairie fires, until heaven and earth roared in one blaze; during the winter she would let loose all the deviltry she could think of, by way of raging blizzards, spewing out a horror of snow and cold. But all in vain; the houses reared themselves faster than she could destroy them. Even the elements had to learn that the power of man had to be respected, especially when energized by a great joy.''

For a while Per Hansa, apparent conqueror of the plain, lacks the strength to contend with the ominous and incessant forebodings of Beret. It takes more than muscle to withstand fears that only intellect can dispel. The great joy that comes with the birth of Peder restores him. Immediate and overwhelming disaster is averted. The newcomer brings an assurance that the monster of the plains cannot always prevail. But Beret's blended orthodoxy and superstition drive Per Hansa out in the blizzard in search for a cleric to perform extreme unction for a dying relative. He goes in vain defiance of the monster and never returns. At last Beret regains her sanity with the aid of the final folk element to enter the tale, the primitive faith embodied in the parson, spokesman of God in whose voice is heard the reassurance of the intercessor. She is reserved for a less elemental chapter in the story and for a less elemental, though no less unqualified, defeat.

Analysis expresses itself in abstract terms; art, with the concrete. Critical analysis is bound, therefore, for the moment to do violence to the object of its attention. Yet the harsh process must be followed a step farther in a word of summary. *Giants in the Earth* is a twofold story. I have tried to suggest the essentials of the first part in terms of primitive ethnology: man and nature in their eternal conflict; man as part of the tide of human life inexorably sure of success; man, the individual, ephemeral as the grass of the field. In "The Land Taking" the conflict is presented, the sentence is pronounced alike on human strength and human weakness, but Peder Victorious is born. Man falls in the taking of the land, but his seed survives for "The Founding of the Kingdom."

The second part becomes a more complicated and sophisticated tale of community life, not to be interpreted in the same terms— no longer recounting a conflict with nature or primitive fears, predestined to ultimate success, but pursuing the later problem of whether man who can subdue the monster of the plain can also adjust his own nature to the stream of circumstance. It is a connecting link with the second volume, the story of Peder himself.

The Grand Canyon yawns no deeper than the chasm between successive generations with its opposing walls of convention and revolt. Between the parents and children of immigrant stock it is wider than normal, even when the newcomers share the language of the new country. But when there is the added cleavage of speech, the abyss sometimes becomes too broad for any but the most tenuous of bridges. *Peder Victorious* tells of this tragic alienation of mother and child. Intimacy is denied them: he cannot understand her songs; he cannot take the nourishment on which her soul has thriven. And more poignant than his loss is hers, for she sees him slip away into an alien fastness where she may not follow because she has not the key and cannot learn the password.

The concluding picture in *Giants in the Earth* is of Per Hansa in the horrid dissolution of death, struck down by the monster of the plain. The concluding scene in *Peder Victorious* is of mother Beret, bending to the inevitable. Her son, promise of the future, is advancing to meet it, speaking the strange tongue of a new land, marrying a strange offspring of another land, their son to be

American born of American born. For Beret there is no alternative but resistance that will lead to total estrangement or acceptance of his choice, and the decision is inevitable. Once more, and in another way, the pioneer is overcome, even while in the act of creating a new America.

Only to this point has Rölvaag brought the chronicle with the completion of *Peder Victorious*. The second immigrant generation has reached its majority; its adult career is still to be faced. This chapter has been written, too, by Martha Ostenso in *Wild Geese;* but her treatment of the story differs as markedly from Rölvaag's as Bojer's does from the earlier stages. For she represents youth, and Rölvaag speaks for both youth and age. He is tolerant of youth and compassionate for age; she is the voice of intolerant rebellion. Caleb Gare, fearful product of pioneering days, is a merciless archfiend with an insatiable lust for land and power and with no grand desires to redeem it. He is "a spiritual counterpart of the land, as harsh, as demanding, as tyrannical as the very soil from which he draws his existence." The planting and tilling season is a "terrific, prolonged passion"; and, like every great passion, while it is at its height it is oblivious to anything beyond itself, forgetful of any aim, regardless of any obstacle.

Miss Ostenso is not quite able to convey her meaning through sheer narrative. Her two young lovers stop to expound her thesis in the middle of the story: "Life here at Oeland may seem a negation, but it is only a reflection from so few exterior natural objects that it has the semblance of negation. These people are thrown in upon themselves, their passions stored up, they are intensified figures of life with no outward expression—no releasing gesture."

"Yes," says the other, "there's no feeling left after the soil and the live-stock have taken their share." And they talk about books. Not only that, but they find their own solution not in any victory over these conditions but in escape from them; and as the author sends them back to urban life from which she has brought them as transient observers of the actual pioneer stock, she kills off the villain of the piece by trapping him in a bottomless swamp while a brush fire sweeps out of control and destroys his finest, unreaped crop.

It remains, then, for Rölvaag or some one like him to face the question from which Miss Ostenso turns with her characters. Not all the later generations of immigrant stock can abandon the soil. What is left to those who remain on it? What will happen to Peder and his like? What does happen to them? They are the new Americans who have sloughed off the ways and traditions of Europe. Their own are in the making; and they are making them in Gopher Prairie, in Winesburg, in Zenith, in Spoon River, just as farther east they are remaking them in Robert Frost's region north of Boston or in Robinson's Tilbury. This problem of America in the making or America coming of age is the problem of universal speculation among all who are putting their minds on the facts of the day or the prospects for day after tomorrow. A typical observation will serve from Waldo Frank's *The Rediscovery of America*.

"In physics, we learn, the energy of motion has the dominant trend to become heat. This is called 'entropy.' In man the energy of Power flows into the need of comfort. This psychologic entropy may not be reversed. Power, with its inherent stages of fatigue, sterility, inner emptiness, passivity, turns to the lust for comfort. But the lust for comfort does not energize fresh power. The child of the Power-man is very often the comfort-seeker; but the outcome of his cult is not more Power. An instance of this 'entropy' is the American scene. We start as hard expositors of Power; we become soft consumers of comfort. But the means of this comfort are not created by the followers of the cult; they are the product still of the men of Power. And a large part of the exercise of Power consists in the selling of 'comfort-devices'—mechanical, political, ideal—to those who already passed into the state of essentially comfort-seekers."

So, for such a truth-teller as Rölvaag, I can

see only two dominant possibilities in the remaining chronicles of Peder: the soil is subdued; a truce has been declared between his mother and himself—the immigrant pioneer and her offspring. The perils he faces are in the people who surround him with their lust for tuppeny-ha'penny prosperity and petty comfort. The monster of the plains no longer intimidates them. A greater menace is the disapproval of the community for whom the seventh and succeeding deadly sins are to disturb the market or the sanctity of the Republican party, to tamper with a vague and unknown something they call the "Constitution," to depart from a literal interpretation of the early chapters of the book of Genesis, or to grant others the slightest indulgence in any of these indulgences or blasphemies.

If in the face of these social orthodoxies, as Peder's story goes on, he stands for the magnanimities and sees life in the large, he will be in for a grinding between the upper and nether millstones that smug conservatism substitutes for the mills of the gods. He may save his soul, but he will be an outcast. Or, on the other hand, if he adjust himself to his barn and his silos and his barbed wire and windmill and tractors, avoids conflict, and makes his little fortune, he will make it at the price of his soul. So the potential tragedy of Peder in the evolving world of security and comfort-seeking may be quite as devastating as the tragedies of Per Hansa or Beret. It is the inevitable consequence of drafting the energies of a whole generation for the promotion of material ends. There must be some valid relation between this and the fact that the country has been spun on a pivot so that the erstwhile wild and woolly West has become the impregnable fortress of tidy conservatism.

One thinks back to Crèvecoeur's unfulfilled prophecy of a new race fused from the nations of the Old World, new men acting on new principles, entertaining new opinions, forming new opinions. It is true, as the rhapsodist predicted, that the American that was to come has caused great changes in the world. Maybe the rest will be true some day short of the millennium. In the meanwhile the fusing process is still on, and the crucible proves to be anything but a bed of roses. And that is why the honest teller of frontier tales—who undertakes neither to idealize nor to prophesy, but simply to portray—is bound to be a somber recorder of the successive conquests of the pioneer.

CHAPTER V

THE BACK-TRAILERS IN FACT AND FICTION

❖

"We go Eastward to realize History," said Thoreau, "retracing the steps of the race."

ONE spring when I was first thinking along the byways followed in these pages, a deep gash was cut through the campus that I cross. From the footwalk alongside I could see odd markings like the faded undulations on an old-fashioned "marbled" book cover. Standing there one twilight with a geologist, I heard him read them: first the present layer of soil, then a gray seeped-out stratum, then the underlying sand; then, dipping a little, a repetition of these three layers; below these in the shape of a quarter-moon, the record of a tiny, ancient swamp. Ancient to the layman, but not to the geologist. "All very recent," he said, "certainly within the last ten thousand years."

A few weeks later I was on another university campus just where the plains and the Rockies meet. It was a beautiful and beautifully permanent-looking garden spot. The older buildings were as ugly as the average of American college architecture, and the newer ones as fine as the best. There were high trees, bold ravines, a lily pond, and rich lawns watered under a blazing sun by a controlled flood whose source could be seen in a glacier back among the mountains. It helped me understand what the psalmist from the arid East had in mind when he said, "I will lift up mine eyes unto the hills whence cometh my help." It made me feel that this seat of learning, presided over by a classical scholar, was founded in antiquity. And then they explained that two generations ago those uplands and hillsides were untouched by the white man.

And that in turn renewed my understanding of the lines that Emerson composed as a descendant of a former frontiersman, when,

looking back eight generations to his fore-
bear, Peter Bulkeley, he wrote,

> Here is the land,
> Shaggy with wood,
> With its old valley,
> Mound and flood.
> But the heritors?—
> . . . .
> They called me theirs,
> Who so controlled me;
> Yet every one
> Wished to stay, and is gone,
> How am I theirs,
> If they cannot hold me,
> But I hold them?

Concord, Massachusetts; Chicago, Illinois;
Boulder, Colorado; or any one of them, con-
tain the three substantial factors of human
history: the permanent earth, the continuing
social order, the passing individual.

The earth is constant enough to lend an
illusive sense of security in spite of air, fire,
and water—dust-drift, eruption, and erosion.
We talk of *terra firma* while we set up wind-
breaks and breakwaters, build dikes, dams,
and flood basins, and hope for the best in the

face of earthquake and volcanic outburst. Secure from brontosaurus, mammoth, and mastodon, we regard ourselves as lords of creation, forget that Tyndall's allusion to "the murderous dominion" of our bacterial foes still contains more truth than fiction, and ignore that in the temperate zones man is carrying on an only moderately successful warfare with the arthropod insects, which are in complete domination of the most fertile regions of the earth. Yet, as there are no insect lawyers to dispute title with us of the habitable regions, and as we have domesticated a half-dozen of the animals and still find some practical use for the cow and the hen, we take the earth as our standard of stability and quaintly think of ourselves as its possessors.

We are not quite so certain as to the permanence of the social order. We are beginning to recognize at least that the experiment of civilization is still in its beginnings and that the inevitability of change is the one law of which we can be sure. The "remote antiquity" of the archaeologist is a term only for temporal provincials. Over the habitable parts of the earth trickles the thin stream of human life adapting itself to its environment, and its environment to itself—always changing. The latest of inventions, the modern American city, is nothing but a chambered nautilus, spreading, casting off its old shells, building itself more stately mansions, turning the old mansions into boarding-houses, the old meeting-houses into warehouses, the old farmhouses into suburban manors, busied with zoning systems that will establish some sort of control, a semblance of order. A recent type of residential architecture has acknowledged itself as a symbol of the times—"permanesque," guaranteed not to endure. As why should it, when city-planners declare that the life-expectancy of a skyscraper is twenty-nine years? America, with its wealth and its energy, can repeat this not as an excuse for starting no more skyscrapers but as a part of the ground-breaking ceremonials. "Twenty-nine years! Almost as long as back to 1900. We should worry! Maybe in twenty-nine more years the cities will be triple-decked, and all the workers will play mole as they go to and from their work in sub-sub-sub-ways. And if the citadels of business crash through the honeycomb of low-ways, we'd soon be pulling them down if they did not fall."

Moreover, if the American wearies of New York or Chicago he can escape on his own wheels to Middletown. There is a smooth ribbon of concrete that he may roll across. America has spent the money for him, ten thousand dollars for every minute of his drive. Middletown, to be sure, is not the town it was twenty-nine years ago. In the old days it used to listen to sermons and lectures, had a zest for rotund eloquence. Now it is too restless to sit through more than brief remarks. Then the library had less than twenty periodicals; now it offers more than two hundred, most of them filled with fiction that provides an escape from Middletown. Middletown used to be on the theatrical "road," and the family could see two or three dozen full-length plays in the course of a winter. Now it is reduced to the moving-picture program with fifty minutes as the maximum length of the feature film. The town has more contacts with music of every kind than it used to, but makes much less melody for itself. The motor car has multiplied the radius of the town by ten; but competition for its use has driven a wedge into the family, and increasing freedom of movement has broken up the old neighborhood bonds. People do not "drop in" as they used to; the "sociable" has gone into the discard; the lodge is losing its grip; dancing demands a hall and a "peppy" orchestra. Organization is taking hold of leisure; the women pursue culture in bands; the town rallies around the high-school basket-ball coach; Rotary, Kiwanis, and Lions combine mutual promotion with the gospel of doing good; and the golf club affords an acreage for exercise and a field for establishing useful business connections. Middletown, coziest village of the plain, is no more. The old swimming-hole is polluted from the factory; the chamber of commerce recommends making White River white again, but rests content with the formulation of a slogan.

West of Middletown the big cities and the transformed towns are re-enacting what took place earlier in the East. The frontier is filled; frontiersmen are known only as "surviving veterans." There is no chance for the small miner now. There is a "king" for every kind of metal, and the operations are on as large a scale as the fortunes that result from them. The small cattle-owner disappeared before the small miner did, and the packers have supplanted the kings. Now the small farmer is listening to his sentence. He has never succeeded in combining with his fellows; as soon as a little friendly legislation is carried into a practice, the national chamber of commerce loses its temper at interference with the methods of the exploiter. Machinery replaces the laborer on the soil; the farmer's son makes for the city to fill the vacuum produced by restricted immigration; the wealthier farmers and city financiers continue to accumulate great tracts and to set up industrial units; and the man with a fertile

quarter-section who does not have to sell out
or hire out or get out has the makings in him
of a magnate who will one day be confront-
ing others with this triple choice.

So, on the land that we choose to think of
as permanent, because any other thought is
too uncomfortable, the social order shifts in
spite of the beneficiaries who like to think of
it as established, because any other thought
is altogether intolerable. Some succeed and
stay where they scored their successes; some
succeed and go East to spend their fortunes.
For the rest there is a new word, a charita-
bly conceived one—maladjustment. It offers
an excuse and partial explanation for the
older and harsher word—failure. And it
accounts also for the people who felt that
they were in the wrong region, whose repugnance to the frontier would probably
have led to defeat and surely to discontent,
and who have sought safety and happiness in
retreat to the older settled country.

It is in the nature of his case that the back-
trailer cannot figure as a hero. If he has not
managed to meet the frontier on its own

terms or to force the frontier to meet his, he
may have been wise to retreat from it; but at
best he has only shown the discretion that is
the less admirable part of valor. And if he
has made his fortune as a power man and is
willing to subside into an eastern comfort-
seeker, he becomes a nabob who never can
win for himself the status that his wealth
will probably confer on his grandchildren.
Not all the perfumes of Arabia can quell the
odors of saddle leather and blasting-powder.
Sheer ostentation lays him open to the
damning innuendos of the élite. A senator
thinking of founding a university asks how
much Harvard is worth, and hearing it is
only fifty million, says to his wife, "I guess
we can afford it." That marks both the beginning of a university and the social finish
of a senator. Another senator, a copper king,
builds himself a frightful and frightfully expensive palace on Fifth Avenue; and the
beautiful twin palaces of a third generation
of railroad magnates a few blocks away hold
him up to daily scorn. These pilers-up of
show-houses and indiscriminate buyers of

art objects have been too obvious to gain much attention in serious literature.

There is Mrs. Wharton's Undine Spragg, to be sure, most memorable of her type, incorrigible product of Apex. She is handsome enough and energetic enough to make temporary conquests in New York and Paris, but the "custom of the country" is far too strong for her to conquer and far too subtle for her to achieve. Henry James's "The American" is a better character, the first real character of the sort. He has thrived in the West and at middle age hungers quite honestly for what his wealth might fitly enjoy: a distinguished home and a distinguished wife to preside over it. He has a vague sense of what it should be and a deeply vague yearning for it. He finds the desirable woman in France, and he is desirable to her; but they both realize before it is too late that centuries of tradition cannot marry a single lifetime of performance, because neither could make the other feel at home. It is one of the finest, truest stories that James ever wrote.

William Dean Howells must be included in

the picture though he does not quite fit into it. In his own experience he seems more of a back-trailer than he was in reality; for though he was born and bred in the frontier days of the Middle West, his family life was rooted in an older culture and his father was a frontier journalist rather than a typical frontiersman. Howells, as a young reporter in Columbus, enjoyed the town not for its activities but as a place where he could talk literature; and after his valuable years in Venice he found himself rather more at home in Boston. From this vantage point, and later from New York, he looked at Europe and at the Middle West with equal detachment. In more than twenty of his stories he brought his westerners to the East or shipped them across the Atlantic. But except for his reminiscent feeling for their first embarrassments with proper dress and their ignorance of some of the amenities, he treated them consciously as an easterner. He even wrote from the point of view of the native New Yorkers "to whom the existence of the vulgar Four Hundred is a matter of supreme indifference." Yet for a long while he betrayed himself by a somewhat conscious awareness of the nuances of eastern behavior, commenting on westernisms that he had escaped from. There is a touch of pharisaism, certainly of the *nouveau*-easterner, in his strictures on the *nouveau-riche*:

"People like the Ralstons come to New York simply because they have got too rich to stay at home, and because they think they can spend their money more agreeably here than where they made it. . . . . They come to New York in the hope of getting their money's worth of whatever they dream of buying here. . . . . The men might be satisfied to remain at home in the castles or palaces that they seem always to build in their first opulence, to overawe the imaginations of their fellow-townsmen; but for their womenkind to be in, if they cannot be of, the metropolis, they leave their local supremacy behind, their great mansions, galleries, greenhouses, libraries of first editions, their whole undisputed state among people who envy it if they do not revere them, and come here, and accept seats far below the salt at the second table or third. . . . . Coming here with their ten or twenty millions, they cannot disabuse themselves of the infatuation in which they have lived at home that they are persons of social consequence."

In these earlier reactions to the back-trailer with the long purse, Howells was unconscious of being, as Aldrich described himself, not really Boston, but only Boston-plated. Later, when a kind of alchemy had taken place in him and he had become completely easternized, he came to acknowledge, like James, that "the Hub" was extraordinarily provincial, and that western influence had helped to free the East from always looking over its shoulder at Europe instead of cultivating its native genius in its native idiom. Yet in his long array of portraits from the Ellisons to the Dryfooses, and from the Dryfooses to the Kentons, he was bearing witness to the fact that, given riches and leisure, the frontier could not be sufficient to itself. Its natural impulse was to look over its shoulder at the East just as the East was doing at Europe; and as soon as it had money and the time for spending, it was tempted to take the first train for New York.

However, the term "back-trailer," as Hamlin Garland has given it to us, applies most definitely to those of the second generation whose repugnance to the frontier is coupled with the memory that they themselves never chose to brave it. It is the city man with farm-boy recollections who has no hankerings to putter with a garden. He leaves that form of play to his friends who have not suffered from it in youth. Howells left the Middle West and looked back on it with friendly interest. John Hay, on the other hand, was almost hostile. He left it in spirit when he went east to college as a boy of seventeen. He was embarrassed and half-ashamed at the "absurd vogue" of his "doggerel" *The Pike County Ballads;* asked Stedman to omit "Little Breeches" from his anthology, explaining that the editor would pardon the request if he only knew how "odious the very name of that hopeless fluke" was to the shamefaced author; urged his friends to read his *Castilian Days;* omitted from his complete poetical works all but three poems with any reference to the West, and if he had re-entitled them could have located them just as well in Spain or Palestine or Paradise, where his fancy loved to rove. A series of letters written from Illinois in the few months after his graduation from a Rhode Island college have been published under the title *A Poet in Exile.* They reveal his refusal to share the pioneer enthusiasm of his father, and a repugnance for frontier conditions which may have come partly from his involuntary experience of them and partly from a remoter ancestral strain.

"My father, with more ambition and higher ideals than I, has dwelt and labored here a life time, and even this winter does not despair of creating an interest in things intellectual among the great unshorn of the prairies. I am not suited for a reformer. . . . . I love comfortable people. I prefer, for my friends, men who can read. In spite of the praise that you continually lavish upon the West, I must respectfully assert that I find only a dreary waste of heartless materialism where great and heroic qualities may indeed bully their way up into the glare, but the flowers of existence inevitably droop and wither."

Soon after this he emerges in a letter from Thomas Wentworth Higginson. It is at a picnic outside of Washington, "got up for a young Mr. Hay," who, it appears, was painfully conscious of his youth, and spent the afternoon "laboring not to appear new-mown" and not to appear as western as the president whose secretary's secretary he was. As the years went on he succeeded in outliving every suggestion of field and farm, so that a later middle-western president, McKinley, referred to him in almost envious admiration as a conservatory product, a fine flower of civilization.

It is apparent by this time, of course, that the good writing about the frontier has come from men and women who have known it at first hand, and that the best of it has come from those who were more than reporters.

The material on the shock troopers of the West was the richest source for the frontier novel. Recent fiction, as we have witnessed, has made good use of this. But the sober and negative experience of the back-trailer has been, so far, left for only one or two. This is not for lack of writers who have known the story at first hand. Most of the writers who came out into the Mississippi Valley, and very many who were born there, have not been content to stay: Howells and Hay; Eggleston and Mark Twain and Bret Harte; Markham and Masters; Ezra Pound, John Gould Fletcher, T. S. Eliot, Ernest Hemingway. The list could be spun out much longer. It is rather that the story is not an easy one to tell, for it must be composed in a minor key; it has no big crescendos and can be hardly more than a sustained anticlimax. Wescott, near the beginning of his career, and Garland, toward the end of one, have dealt most effectively with it.

Garland prepared the ground for it in *A Son of the Middle Border*, started the actual chronicle of it in the second volume of this (which his publishers prevailed on him to misname *A Daughter*), and concluded it explicitly in the final instalment, *Back-Trailers from the Middle Border*. What might be regarded as a dreary and unsignificant account of semi-defeat has a large measure of significance because of its genuinely epic quality. There are a good many personal elements in the narrative that may as well be, and easily can be, forgotten. Though Mr. Garland seems not to have been quite enough of a spendthrift to be gaily improvident, his financial worries after his recurrent extravagances need not worry the reader. He was ill and despondent for some years, and the story of that period is overshadowed by aches and pains and depressions and discouragements; but as he passed his three-score-and-ten mark he was neither invalid nor insolvent, he had known honor, love, obedience, troops of friends, and he was more to be envied than pitied.

The choice of the back trail is essentially interesting only as it involves characters of some potential significance. The featureless victim of circumstance may be dimly pathetic; but if he shows no capacity for combat and no inclination to choose for himself, he can hardly evoke much active sympathy. There is a shadowy figure in the middle of the three volumes of autobiography—Burton Babcock, who followed the western movement clear to the Klondike, and thrived there no better than he had in the Middle Border. He lived out his last years as camp cook and night watchman, but in these years he reached "a lofty serenity which approached content." Slight as his part is in the history, it is moving and meaningful because there is something positive about it. The conquest of new territory in the name of civilization is carried on by an unthinking army, the rank and file in which are more instruments than agents. They show incredible endurance and courage; but they are swept on by some impulse to which, even though they may have voluntarily submitted, they are blindly, dumbly obedient. In the days of limited military enlistment there used to be moments for redecision. And the necessity for choice between return home or return to the ranks tugged at hesitant recruits with the same alternative pulls that have confronted the back-trailer.

The man on the postfrontier at the passing of the century, if he had misgivings of any kind, was sure to have more than one kind. On the one hand was an open dissatisfaction with conditions in a district where the first heroic campaign was over, where the heroes of the campaign were passing into dependent old age, and where there was no new enthusiasm for life or for vigorous performance. The little towns were drab and ugly. There was no desire to beautify them or to beautify life in them. In the midst of such circumstances the alien immigrant had no choice, he had made an irrevocable one; but the American found that this very choice was forcing him into a new dilemma—that of being an alien among aliens, a stranger on American soil, or, his pioneering now over, of taking the back trail.

If, then, he felt, as Garland did, that he had tastes which could be better gratified in the older settlements and powers that could be better spent there, he might join the centripetal movement of the day and justify himself by saying that he belonged as much to the present as his father did to the past. He could point to all the other men of his kind who had preceded him in the same direction. He could pull up stakes and set out for the East. Yet, even then, the West would continue to drag at his heartstrings. He would find himself softening for lack of exercise, chafing at dust and soot and noise, longing for the roominess of the country, for an acreage instead of a fire escape, for a big stove instead of a gas log, for the sound of wind in the trees and the odors of new-mown hay and burning leaves. More poignant than these losses would be the never-dying sense of vague disloyalty to his ancestry, to the men of power from whom he sprang. Ought he to have left the region they had conquered? But again, should he demand that his wife return there, and could he demand that his children partake of his childhood, instead of a richer one than he could provide them in a western town? "There are people," he might say, as did Garland, "there *must* be people who still love to farm, to milk cows, to pick fruit and to dig potatoes—how else can we go on eating? [a rather facile begging of the question] but such doings are not for me. I have had my share of such activities. I am content to feed my goldfish and exercise my small dog on the roof. I do not intend to play the hypocrite in this matter, urging the other fellow to go west, as Horace Greeley did, while enjoying Times Square and upper Broadway myself."

He convinces himself in this fashion, humanly searching for a principle after he has arrived at a decision, and even goes so far as to declare that the best service he can do for the region he has abandoned is to represent it with distinction, thus reflecting credit on it from a comfortable distance. He is near the market for his wares, for he is literary, and editors will take what they will not ask for, and telephone for what they will not request by mail. And he is among birds of his feather and can twitter or chirp or crow with them as they feed together, and go back to his desk and scratch the better for the friendly talk. And meanwhile there are the concerts and the plays and the dinners that he and his fellow-authors are invited to sit at and speak at and lend luster to and be reported as gracing; and rich friends as well as talented ones—friends with cars and yachts and country places and illimitable hospitality, who are as proud to entertain distinction as distinction is generous in conferring itself when the price is only the acceptance of luxuries. All of which is good for the soul, and for the waistband, and for one's family, and highly educative for the youngsters. Who may say that a man should withhold these benefits from those he loves?

But then there come new complications into the changing life—for certainly it is no small change that has been elected. Back on the frontier one was all for simplicity, making a virtue of necessity. Those were the days, still vividly rememberable, when one scorned a dress suit as "the livery of privilege" worn only by the predatory rich and

their servants. Garland considers the possibility of making this concession. Eugene
Field's prospective derision makes it the
harder, but Howells eases it by suggesting
"the inexorability of English social usages."
Moreover, he decides, there is much in pag-
eantry. If one should maintain "*mens sana in
corpore sano*," why not *corpus sanum* in proper
garb? Ultimately, one sits at Carnegie's table
undistinguishable in dress from all the other
guests as well as from the waiters. Evening
clothes have become a symbol of democracy.
Nor is this all. Wealth, which one hated and
distrusted from the disadvantage point of the
frontier, becomes amiable at closer range. It
turns out to have ennobling qualities. One
not only comes to approve it in general but
even arrives at the stage of abandoning the
condemnation of "intangible wealth" in
stocks and bonds, and happily invests the
proceeds from the sale of Oklahoma lands.
The ex-frontiersman clips his coupons with
quiet joy in the impressive security of a safe-
deposit crypt beneath a gorgeous bank and
expands with confidence in his emancipation

from the tyranny of the sky. Fear of the weather dies; the hot winds of Dakota and the blizzards of Oklahoma sink into dim memories of a poverty-stricken past.

Moreover, the thought of evening clothes as symbols of democracy is tinged with the humor of Louis XIV when he dressed his lackeys in the court costume of Charles II. The back-trailer is no longer irreconcilably committed to republicanism. He admits that there is no enjoyment in losing himself in the mob, no thrill in the sight of the army of garment workers catching their midday breath on lower Fifth Avenue. "But to see a duke in a golden coach, or a prince in historic armor lends a pleasurable momentary distinction to the humble onlooker. No matter how lowly we are, we share in the rays of his glory, just as each tiny leaf and bud derives a grateful transitory gleam from the passing of the sun."

This leads nearer the heart of the matter. The back-trailer yearns for the city and turns to the East, but he turns to the East because it is the avenue to the past. He summers in

London with his family once and again, and revels in the sense of ancient dignities. He has none of Mark Twain's insistence that the American abroad should not defer to everything European or pretend to deference when he does not feel it. He is altogether as reverent as Mark Twain was among the ruins at Karnak or in the presence of the pyramids. But he is more easily satisfied. Any pageant is a symbol of antiquity, and antiquity is something to revere. The Connecticut Yankee was a blasphemer when he jeered at King Arthur's court. The elder days should never be stripped of the glamor of romance. If pushed to a defense this back-trailer might quote his Emerson: "Nevertheless Romance is Mother of Knowledge. . . . . If the unknown was not magnified, nobody would explore. Europe would lack the regenerating impulse and America would lie waste, had it not been for El Dorado." The back-trailer, completing the circuit, seeks his El Dorado in the lands from which the first pioneers set forth in search of theirs. It is the return of the prodigal son, sure of his food, and cured of his restless discontent. A young and zealous pioneer clansman, he once blazed with the zeal of a reformer and fought the exploiters who were obstructing the millennium. But with old age nearing much faster than the millennium, he frankly makes for ease and security. The frontier has been despoiled in any case, the age of pioneering is gone and with it the magic is gone out of the West. The older regions offer beauty and the peaceful gratification of the senses. He takes refuge in entrenched conservatism. The son of the power man is become a complacent comfort-seeker. And in this he finds a measure of contentment. This is some distance from a fulfilment of Howells's wish expressed in 1894: "Garland . . . . is taking on the world ingenuously and interestingly; he will never be sophisticated, and I hope he won't lose the simplicity of his ideal, such as it was when he had 'Main Traveled Roads' under his feet, and throbbed with his fine, angry sympathy for 'the familiar and the low.' "

The purpose of this study is more historical than critical. The question that rises from such a statement of events is not whether it is admirable but whether it is true. Many people have passed through some such experience. It is a part of recent history even though it is not true of all pioneers or even of all back-trailers.

Glenway Wescott supplements it with another story which has more to do with establishing a state of mind and less to do with immediate circumstances and associations. To Garland life is an objective experience. He plowed and milked and sweated as a husky boy. He journeyed east over memorable miles. He studied and starved in chill rooms in Boston. He traveled and wrote and went in and out of editorial offices and hobnobbed with innumerable people in all kinds of picturesque settings. To think of his books is to think of definite events happening in definite settings and to recall definite aspirations that were always connected with specific conditions of living. It is the experience of the realist.

Wescott in *The Grandmothers* recounts the

experience of the romanticist. A young westerner of the third generation finds himself
looking back at life in the same Wisconsin
where Garland was born and bred. He is
grown up, as the saying goes, but to him
there is nothing definitive in that. He wonders what he has grown up to and what he
has grown up from. From his own heritage
he cannot escape. It fascinates him to the
point of an obsession. He is an incarnation,
and he dwells on the lives of his forebears in
a kind of extended introspection. From the
region, however, he may free himself. Its
past, "a wilderness of history and hearsay,"
need not be his; it is merely the studio in
which the portraits of the family were
painted and where they still hang. He never
really participated in its active life. He has
not had either the physique nor the inclination for hard labor, and necessity has not
driven him to it. He knows that he never
could have endured the comfortless glory of
his pioneer grandparents. Money that one of
the Towers had married made schooling possible for him, and early escape into Chicago.

Yet, in the story, he is a Tower himself; and he realizes, perhaps as none of the first of them did, that what he has inherited from them are the traits that doomed them to non-success on the frontier.

They were slight of build; even what their backs might have lifted their hands could never grip. They were sensitive and unassertive and scrupulous in the ways that withheld them from a fierce entrance into a free-for-all scramble. They had seen churlish, clumsy men shoulder them aside. They cherished a grievance against this common clay and felt superior in defeat. Into their young literary descendant have passed creative vanity that brought forth little, and fruitless pride that fed upon itself. What chance for the fringe of aristocracy on the fringe of civilization? There had been so little hope for them that its fulfilment was little indeed.

Now the changed conditions confront him with a question. What is his place? What his obligations? His people were pioneers because their dispositions unfitted them for anything else without fitting them for this desperate alternative. His own alternatives are hardly less desperate. Shall he undertake in his generation to make something for the future out of this struggle which has left the Middle Border breathless and sweaty and still rapacious? The future of America depends on his generation. But he has looked upon the past of America until his discoveries have revealed too much and robbed him of courage. "Indeed, it was an instinctive law for Americans, the one he had broken. Never be infatuated with, nor try to interpret as an omen the poverty, the desperation of the past; whoever remembers it will be punished, or punish himself; never remember. Upon pain of loneliness, upon pain of a sort of expatriation, though at home. At home in a land of the future where all wish to be young."

He goes abroad and one day comes back for Christmas with his family in the home town. It is a new town, newer than the farms that surround it. The houses are planted on the earth but not anchored to it, wooden tents.

The manners of the people there are unsettled. There have been changes in the church, in the college. Men who want things done are pulled between the challenges of the younger generation and the conservatisms of the elder. This is true elsewhere, but here the irresolution is the greater because of the lack of either settled traditions or articulate desires. The whole Middle West seems to him to suffer from the "nervousness of vagabonds who have no native land left. . . . . There is no Middle West. It is a certain climate, a certain landscape; and beyond that, a state of mind of people born where they do not like to live."

In a few days he turns back to the East again, headed, sooner or later, for a return to Europe. He says *Good-Bye, Wisconsin* in a book that is filled with the yearnings and defeats of this region which in the life of its nation represents neither youth nor age. It is melancholy to leave, for he knows that democracy is coming to some sort of climax and that his generation, those whose birthrights have set them more to doing than to thinking, will soon be claiming the powers and the rewards of the lords of the earth. But for himself, he wishes he could write a book about ideal people living in ideal circumstances, where outer harmony and beauty prevail and where only the ineluctable trials of the spirit can intrude; and he would like so to write it that he and his origins and his prejudices and his Wisconsin will all disappear. When he has done this, he will ask himself whether he has chosen the way of the courageous, and he will stand self-condemned. He is an expatriate because the struggle to be a middle westerner or an American and to be honest at the same time is too much to demand of him.

This is not a passage for the hundred per cent American to read; but no one of that stripe will have come this far. Wescott's portrait is just as typical as Garland's. Wescott's decision for his character is no different from Henry James's or of fifty other distinguished Americans from Benjamin West to John Sargent, from Crèvecoeur to Stephen Crane. Mark Twain kept silence and took vengeance posthumously on "the damned human race"; Ambrose Bierce disappeared in Mexico; Lafcadio Hearn waned in Japan. Ezra Pound, John Gould Fletcher, T. S. Eliot, have fled to England or the Continent. It is the final word in reaction against the life that the pioneers left as their melancholy legacy. Vague optimism accepts this, militant energy converts it into something finer; but the ways of the back-trailer are not followed to their extreme until they are followed to the final resort of the expatriate. And Wescott is their interpreter.

CHAPTER VI

IMPLICATIONS

✧

THE rivalry between fact and sentiment is ceaseless in the literature of the frontier because it is native to the subject and native to humankind. We look away for agreeable prospects, for we know that distance blends and softens what might be ugly at hand. When the frontier was still a reality, the temptation to idealize it was strongest. It was a land of hope and promise, a place of escape from the drudgery of here and now. It was comforting to many a man who never sought it. Routine stayed tolerable so long as the door and gate were open; discontent became reconciled to the bleakness of the New England farm, the noise in the factory, the listlessness at desk or counter, so long as they were not inevitable.

So the first writer, or the early writer, on the frontier was bound by this preconception. He composed for the man at home, and set his imagination free in a fertile land, full of game, with just enough risk and hardship to offer thrilling adventures and heroic successes. For every one reader who was tempted to convert fiction into fact, a hundred or a thousand settled more snugly by the fireside, enjoying the freedom to stay at home. The frontier served its purpose for a multitude of absentee landlords, soothed by the narcotic of unveracious fiction; and it supplied a salable formula for the writer of popular romance.

But another, more insidious temptation beset the more scrupulous romanticist. He yearned for a happy ending quite as eagerly as his readers. Yet for the average settler the frontier was dreary and the ending was drab. Natural kindliness made it hard for most story-tellers to follow the grim course of events when it could so easily be averted by a stroke of the pen. To reinforce their own tender-heartedness they could fall back on the literary tradition of poetic justice. So they played providence for their favorite characters, and in the closing chapters paid them in cash the rewards which a compassionate theology postpones a stage farther but finally bestows as the earned increment of treasure laid up in heaven.

Furthermore, the teller of frontier tales who aimed at strict realism had his own pitfalls to avoid. It is no slight matter to achieve the truth, the whole truth, and nothing but the truth in a world where black lies are illicitly current and where white ones are sanctioned in the straitest of codes. The attempts in the nineties to present an actual, factual West were made by men with grievances. They were in the position, not of expert witnesses, but of prosecuting attorneys. They were out to make cases against the frontier, its physical hardships, and its social delinquencies; and they made their cases, after the manner of attorneys, by omission, selection, overemphasis, and appeal to emotion. Fact about the frontier could be converted into truth only by the novelist who was both an actual pioneer and an honest artist. That is why only two or three have approached high success and why one is pre-eminent among them.

We began with an allusion to Turner's suggestive essay with its most suggestive title, *The Significance of the Frontier in American History*. A dozen books that have appeared while these pages were being written have reconfirmed his thesis. The best of this crop of 1930, Edna Ferber's *Cimarron*, centers about the last dramatic rush for the free lands—the closing of the frontier. And now that the whole West is explored and the habitable portions are all occupied, the last phase of the cycle appears in those heirs to the labors of the pioneer who will not accept their heritage. It is a tale that is told, a round that is completed. History and literature have recorded all its successive stages. But there still remains the question of the sequel, for history is a serial story, always to be continued. Will it go on to an anticlimax, a series of negations?

The westering movement gave life to much that is most truly American. It held out the promise of peace and plenty. Beyond the horizon, and ever beyond, it offered happy contentment. It ravished the dreamer with the thrilling hope of an earthly paradise, reviving his youth, lending him fresh vigor to reach for what seemed so nearly within his grasp, enriching him in the prospect of what lay beneath the sunset, gilded by its splendor. The promise was not fulfilled. What the pioneer found was less than what he sought; he was fettered by the Old Adam in himself; his past pursued him. But at his best he was stronger for the ordeal. He learned to endure and to attempt the impossible and never to lose hope. In him and the sterner of his offspring is the capacity for a new vision, and perhaps for finding a new America within himself.

It remains for the America of today to conserve this spirit of youth or lose it. On the surface the picture of the moment is a shadowed one. The prophets of evil, who will have none of progress, find plenty on which

to dilate. The foes of the Puritan have themselves become the propounders of natural de-
pravity, while the heirs of Calvinism are
fruitlessly trying to coerce the country into
righteousness by raising the Decalogue to the
tenth power and multiplying sins through
the multiplication of prohibitory laws. But
in the meanwhile, behind all the machinery
of social life, there is a wide-reaching America
that is still mobile, wishful for a general enjoyment of its material advantages, at a
point where it is ready to move from mere
prosperity to the right enjoyment of prosperity, and, above and beyond all, critical of
itself as never before. National self-examination is more than keeping pace with national
complacency. And this healthy fact leads the
prophets of good to concur with the verdict
of so wise an observer as John Dewey when
he writes, "If this new spirit, so unlike that
of old-world charity and benevolence, does
not already mark an attainment of a distinc-
tive culture on the part of American civilization, and give the promise and the potency of
a new civilization, Columbus merely ex-

tended and diluted the Old World. But I still believe that he discovered a New World.''

If we take a last look over the recent literature of the frontier in the search for something more positive than the swan song of the back-trailer, we find it in the pages of Sinclair Lewis. After all the Jeremiads that he poured out so insistently and at last so tediously on the decadent postfrontier, he turned to the other side of the medal, concluding wisely that he had not told the whole story; that life—particularly the life of a district or an era—is never all of one tone, cannot be fairly disposed of in one formula. In witness to which he wrote *Dodsworth*.

Life on the frontier, he recalls at last, demands fortitude. Dumb fortitude may be strong enough not only to survive but also to do the work that the frontier exacts; it may physically conquer a part of the physical world at the loss of its own soul. It may develop the energizing power that can lay out cities and build railroads over the graves of fallen hosts of trail-makers and plowmen. In its planting and its tilling it may raise a sporadic crop from dragons' teeth that yield a harvest of exploiters and Philistines, and these may impose their gospel of success on the less energetic and the less successful. But this is not all that comes from fortitude. Now and again the idealist survives the whole harsh experience of the frontier, beats nature at its own game, and stays blithe; holds his own in the free-for-all scrabble without becoming money-mad; keeps his head and sticks to his own sense of values in spite of the safe-and-sane and the returners to normalcy. And if in the process he has managed to succeed according to the accepted measure of having an excessive number of things that he does not need, he may even be tolerated by the community that does not approve of his views but can't help acknowledging his bank account.

After sacrificing a Babbitt and an Arrowsmith and frustrating a Carol Kennicott, Lewis presents in Sam Dodsworth a man who is strong enough first to succeed and then to withstand success. And he is so completely a product of the best traits of newer America that he resolves to put his wealth and his energy into his own way of doing what he thinks is worth while. True to his character, he does not express himself in establishing an art museum or subsidizing an orchestra; but he goes back to his old work of making automobiles, though a new sort that people can enjoy themselves and go slow in; and he dreams of building beautiful suburbs, authentically American, far enough from the crazy agglomerations of architectural odds and ends that surround most of our cities today.

The whole significance of Dodsworth is that, instead of representing in him just the energy of the frontiersman put to work toward ends that he has never dreamed of, and instead of admiring an insatiable desire for activity as implicitly as the sentimentalists used to admire a quick responsiveness of the lachrymal glands, Lewis makes of this big cub a dreamer who at fifty decides to continue his education, and find out what he is involved in, and keep on dreaming. He is a

Babbitt undefeated, an Arrowsmith with a backbone, for he is big enough to withstand the silly coerciveness of men who are littler than he, and to learn from the men who are bigger. So when Elon Richards, cosmopolite and financial magnate, advises him, after his retirement, to return to the American adventure, "because it is an adventure that we have here—the greatest in the world—and not a certainty of manners in an uncertainty of the future, like all of Europe," he assents. Richards, he concludes, is right: "Our adventure is going to be the bigger because we *do* feel that Europe has a lot we need. We're no longer satisfied with the log cabin and the corn pone. We want everything that Europe has. We'll take it." Dodsworth has already graduated from the school that could mistake the "everything" of Richards' remark for material belongings. He admits his inexperience and sets about to learn from Europe and to keep on growing in wisdom as well as in stature. And in doing this he keeps alive the spirit of the frontier and holds out a promise for the future of America.

[PRINTED
IN U·S·A·]